The Citizen's Guide to Planning

Revised Edition

By Herbert H. Smith

American Planning Association
Chicago
Washington, D.C.

Planners Press, Chicago 60637

Originally published in 1961 as *The Citizen's Guide to Planning,* ©
1961 Chandler-Davis Publishing Company.

First printing, 1961; second printing, 1962; third printing, 1963; fourth
printing, 1964; fifth printing, 1967; sixth printing, 1969; seventh printing, 1972.

To Nancy and Elsie, wife and sister, who by their patient and prodding encouragement have shown more confidence than I deserve, and to Merilee and Tracey, my friends and daughters, who have shown more understanding than I deserve.

Contents

Foreword

As communities are increasingly beset by problems of growth and development, as they struggle to provide essential municipal services without bankrupting themselves, as the great metropolitan areas sprawl ever outward, the realization grows that we must adjust our attitudes toward community organization if we are to preserve traditional values. The word "planning" is increasingly bandied about—but what does it mean?

Unfortunately, there is a lack of common understanding of the meaning of the word. In the minds of most of our citizens, it evokes no clearcut concept: in the jargon of the advertising agency, no image is created. Until very recently, planning activities have too often been confined to mere academic exercises undertaken by professionals, and understood—if at all—only by other professionals. As the emphasis on the rebuilding of the cities and the planning of suburban towns continues to increase, more and more citizens find themselves appointed to planning boards or commissions. Often armed only with good intentions, a vague idea of what planning is all about, and a willingness to learn, the new member of the planning board (the term "planning board" will be used hereafter as synonymous with "planning commission") needs a source of information written in plain language. The purpose of this book is to set forth the meaning of planning in terms understandable by all interested laymen.

It has been my intention to write a book primarily for the newly appointed member of a planning board or a newly interested private citizen, and the book has been organized to cover the areas of planning most likely to be encountered by such a person. To the greatest extent possible, I have avoided technical terminology, statistical formulas, and detailed study outlines. The book is based upon my personal experience and sets forth information obtained and conclusions reached during my participation in some 200 municipal planning programs, a number of county and regional planning projects, and a state planning program.

The observations which follow are based upon the sincere belief that planning is an extremely desirable governmental function, and that the prospects for communities which attempt to face the future without sound planning are frightening to behold. We can and must be better informed on this subject if our efforts to build better communities are not to be wasted.

—from the original "Foreword," April 1961.

When I started this revision of *The Citizen's Guide to Planning*, my intention was to replace my original "Foreword" as outdated. After reflecting about it, I decided, instead, to leave it intact and to comment on it. Rereading what I had written back in 1961 caused me to consider a whole series of questions about our society and our system and about the status of things as they are now compared to our attitudes and condition 10 or 15 years ago. Have we made a better country or a better world? Have we learned from past mistakes, or are we merely repeating our previous ones? Do we have any better understanding of the value of precious resources, the environment, social justice, and orderly development? Have we reached the point at which we understand the difference between exploitation and deriving a fair and just return on private investment that does not demand public subsidy for undue enrichment of selfish interests? Are we able to point with pride to informed, concerned, and responsive leaders and elected officials who put community good above personal interests?

From an entirely cynical viewpoint, one could answer all such questions with a resounding "No," although that might be an unfair generalization. Nevertheless, even the most optimistic among us would have to admit realistically that, while we have made progress in some of the areas of concern, we, the American public, have "been weighed in the balance and found wanting." We have continued to take too much for granted, to assume that technology will solve all of our problems, to consider those who cry out about the rape of our landscape and our resources as "kooks," and to lull ourselves complacently into a false sense of security while being anesthetized by an electronic marvel that projects pictures and sound and succeeds only in turning life into a spectator sport.

It is a certainty that neither this book nor any other is going to change either human nature or a great many attitudes. Even so, after 30 years of frequent frustration over our lack of concern, I continue to hope for the future and have faith in our system and our people. Many have grown in awareness and the voices of our concerned citizens, now much louder, are being heard. Neighborhoods are becoming a rallying point for organization, involvement, and legitimate demands for effective community development and planning. Citizen action groups are finding that well-stated and well-supported positions can be convincingly put forth to affect planned change based upon genuine community interest. In short, there are winds of change—change for the better—blowing on the American scene. It is my hope that my small effort in revising this book can help to keep those winds blowing.

Therefore, I have broadened the purpose of this second edition. While initially I had wanted *The Citizen's Guide to Planning* to be useful to all interested citizens, I directed my first edition largely toward members of planning boards. With the changes that have taken place in our cities and rural areas, with the shift in the direction of planning and, especially, of the federal programs that have been to a large measure the supporting financial base, all of us—not just the members of our elected or appointed bodies—must be informed. We need civic leaders, neighborhood organizers, educators, and young people who are aware that the future, their future, is too important to leave to the work of others or to chance. This book is intended to provide some thought and encouragement to any concerned person who is resolved to be more a part of the future.

At the time I first wrote the book, after having been a practicing planner in both the public and private sectors for 13 years, I am afraid I was convinced there were not many of the "whys" and "wherefores" of planning that I didn't know. It was my belief then, however, and still is now, that planners spend altogether too much time talking to each other and far too little time trying to explain the importance of meaningful planning to the general public. I may never know whether my attempt to present what I then thought I knew was successful at all, even though the book went through seven printings. I do know, having added another 16 years to my professional experience (in private practice and as a city planning director, city manager, and planning educator), that I have come to a stage in life when I realize how little I knew earlier. I also know that I probably have even fewer answers to the question of how effective planning can and should be done now. Hopefully, this can be taken as a sign of maturing. Nevertheless, there is one thing that I knew in 1961 but now know more factually and with an even deeper conviction than I have ever known it: there is no more important problem facing the American people than that of how to make community planning effective in a democratic society.

Finally, I'd like to acknowledge and pay my personal thanks to Dr. Joel B. Goldsteen, Director, City and Regional Planning Program, University of Texas at Arlington, and to Mr. Trafton Bean, Planning Consultant, Boulder, Colorado, for their review and helpful comments, and to Nancy Smith for early editing and correcting and for changing most of the split infinitives.

Herbert H. Smith
Denver, Colorado, 1978

1. The Reasons for Planning

Hundreds of thousands of words are written yearly about human exploitation of natural resources, our misuse of the land, and the increasingly complex organization of our urban communities. Again and again the same conclusion is reached: if order is to be created out of chaos, the solution will be found in the process of planning.

With the development of the automobile, people have gained vastly increased freedom of movement. Their desire to escape from crowded and deteriorating cities has become manifest in the horizontal metropolises of the automobile age. Starting from the central cores of established cities, Americans have expanded outward, first in concentric rings and then along the corridors of major roadways in the pattern often called urban sprawl. In the flight from the city, however, the suburban dweller does not leave behind an aquired taste for the conveniences of city life and desire for organized (and expensive) municipal services. The suburban family wants their children's schools to be well-staffed and efficient. They expect round-the-clock police and fire protection. If garbage and trash are not collected twice a week, they become extremely upset. Frequently, they find themselves so closely crowded against neighbors in a recently rural area that public water and sewerage facilities must be installed to protect the public health. More often than not, new recruits to the open spaces will want the convenience of nearby shopping facilities as well, provided, of course, that the gasoline station or delicatessen isn't built next door to their house.

In the meantime, city dwellers face increasing problems of their own. No longer do they have a stable tax base that permits the provision of adequate municipal services. No longer do they live in the midst of a

large residential complex of solid citizens interested in their community and filled with civic pride. The central business district becomes
more difficult to maintain as trade is lost to suburban shopping centers.
There seems to be no end to the number of cars for which adequate
parking spaces must be found; automobiles clog every major street.
Older residential areas suddenly seem outmoded, deteriorated, even
blighted. Costly corrective measures must be taken, and urban renewal
projects involving the relocation of families, the acquisition of properties, and the clearance and rebuilding of whole blocks at a time seem the
only solution.

PLANNING AND THE TAX BASE

Whether we live in the suburbs or in the city, we are faced with soaring
taxes, an inadequate supply of available housing for all economic
groups, rising crime rates, increasing pollution, inadequate streets and
roads, decreasing services, decaying municipal facilities, and insufficient and inefficient school systems. There is only one way that the
means of meeting the costs of improving the situation can be found:
these funds must come from the money you and I pay in federal, state,
and local taxes. While federal and state aid programs have increased
greatly during the past 20 years, satisfactory services and desirable
amenities, the things that distinguish a good community from just
another blot on the landscape, must still come from one primary
source, the municipal tax base. Unless this tax base is sound and
continually improves, the ever-rising demand for services cannot be
met.

Unfortunately, we have been told that the only way the tax base
can be improved or even maintained is if we do nothing to discourage
all forms of growth, adopt no regulations or restrictions that will
hamper "free enterprise" in any way, and, certainly, never demand that
development be anything more than mediocre. To do otherwise, we are
told, simply will drive away economic opportunities and preclude the
creation of jobs for our people. But will it really? In thinking about
desirable, attractive cities or neighborhoods you have seen—the places
that made you think, "How nice it would be to live there"—what did
you find attractive about them? Was it that their people had no sense of
purpose and direction and left things to chance, being satisfied with

whatever happened, or was it because someone cared, someone bothered to plan, and those involved recognized that quality and excellence are important and can be achieved? If the truth were known, it would be that the residents of desirable neighborhoods have discovered that quality breeds excellence and that, the higher you set your standards, the more you are sought out by those looking to make sound economic investments. One city in the Southwest, with which I was once associated, may have learned this the hard way. Its officials made a zoning change in violation of an adopted future land use plan so that a major industry could locate in an expanding residential area. The space should have been used for a school and open space to add stability to the residences; but the company wanted "freeway exposure," refused to consider other sites in an excellent industrial park already zoned, and threatened to go to another community if they didn't get their way. The change was made, and the plant is now surrounded by a KOA campground and some rather ill-conceived mobile-home parks.

The better cities and the better neighborhoods (and this does not simply mean more wealthy) know that Dr. John R. Silber, president of Boston University, was right when he said in an article on excellence in *Harper's* magazine:

> The only standard of performance that can sustain a free society is excellence. It is increasingly claimed, however, that excellence is at odds with democracy; increasingly we are urged to offer a dangerous embrace to mere adequacy.... Our flight from excellence is profoundly philosophical. Out of a well-intentioned but inept concern with equality of opportunity, we have begun to reject anything that exceeds anyone's grasp. Some might argue that it is our right to engage in this curious flight, and so it is, the right of free men to be fools. But do we have the right as citizens in a free society to reject excellence on behalf of others who may not be so foolish?

Thus, if we are really honest with ourselves, we know that in the area of land and resource utilization, people, if left to their individual devices, will be seduced by the siren of exploitation in our erstwhile "free enterprise" system. Collective society's use of the planning process is the only way that this can be overcome, excellence achieved, the errors of the past corrected, current mistakes avoided, and future misjudgments held to a minimum.

As each new subdivision of land occurs—whether it be for residential, commercial, or industrial purposes—the community of the future takes shape. The use made of the land, the physical organization of the developed area, and the population density after development are the primary determinants of the need for municipal facilities and services. At the same time, only the development of land can provide a substantial enlargement of the real property tax base of the community. Throughout the country, the largest single source of local revenue is the real property tax.

The U.S. Census Bureau reports that of the $67.5 billion that local governments collected from taxpayers in 1976, 81 percent came from property taxes—about 9 percent of Americans' income. The average paid was $266 per property, as compared with $166—an increase of 60 percent. Thus, Californians went to the polls in June of 1978 and passed "Proposition 13" by a better than two-to-one vote to constitutionally limit the taxation on real estate. The taxpayer revolt was off and running.

While in recent years there has been a movement toward minimizing the real estate tax as the prime source of municipal support, it is still the most reliable means available. Tax assessments are based upon values of land and real property improvements, which, in turn, are a reflection of the standards and characteristics of any given area. The logic of insisting upon quality development in these times of municipal financial crisis would appear to be beyond question, except to those whose only objective is speculative personal enrichment. A well-supported citizen-based municipal planning program is the only way, however, that the wisdom of this logic can be applied to governmental structure. Planning for the future development of the community is not only good sense; it is good business.

A PENNY SAVED IS A PENNY EARNED

Logical patterns of land use based upon the needs and desires of individual communities can be established through planning and enforced through zoning. Attractive, carefully developed, orderly communities have inherently sound economic foundations. When we permit haphazard, disorganized, and unattractive development, we allow the destruction of the very essence of sound community life. In effect, we require those citizens who take pride in their property to subsidize the exploitation of the community by the entrepreneur whose sole interest is in a maximum profit from real estate development.

Many examples can be cited to substantiate the practical wisdom of planning for the future. During my private consulting days, I saw a municipality save tens of thousands of dollars through its planning program by anticipating the extension of the municipal sewer system in advance of the construction of a railroad overpass. By arranging for the installation of the necessary sewer pipes (even though they were not to be used immediately) at the time of the construction of the overpass, the municipality saved not only a sizable amount of money but also a great deal of inconvenience.

In another community in which I worked for a number of years, I saw several hundred thousand dollars saved by the careful study and redesign of proposed subdivisions. In many cases, it was possible to reduce the length of streets, resulting in both a lower initial cost for the developer and lower maintenance costs for the municipality. By relating proposed subdivisions to a master plan for future development, the right-of-way for a projected major street was assembled through dedication, at no cost to the municipality.

On the other side of the coin, I saw a city pay $12,000 for a small parcel of land essential to the improvement of a street intersection. Nine years before, the city had acquired the very same parcel through tax delinquency but, in its anxiety to return it to the tax rolls (and in the absence of any long-range plan), had sold the land for $360.

More recently, I was involved in a city that, in order to preserve a scenic mountain backdrop for the public and prevent developers from dotting it with housing, paid $3,000 an acre for 520 acres of land most suited for mountain goats. The irony of this is that, only about 15 years before, this same land had been sold for delinquent taxes for about $50 per acre, the buyers having to pay nothing down, nothing on the principal over the years, and only a very nominal interest rate. The city was not planning conscious and saw no reason at the time to be concerned. Incidentally, the land buyers, most of whom were "pillars" of the community, wanted $7,500 an acre for the land from the city, and it was only by some strong-armed tactics and the threat of public reaction that they were "encouraged" to allow the purchase at the "bargain" price. Endless examples of this kind could be cited, many of them far more expensive to the taxpayer.

No thinking person, I suppose, doubts that a community can save money through sound planning, but one of the most important reasons for planning is intangible. Few of us can say honestly that we are satisfied with the kind of environment we are creating in and around our communities. If we look at the general aspect of our cities, towns, and suburbs, what do we see? Have they been improving, and is life being made more pleasant, enjoyable, sensible, and orderly for our people? Are we eliminating the sore spots of obsolescence and decay, strengthening our central business cores, and overcoming the bottlenecks of traffic and parking? Are we conserving our open space and providing future generations with an opportunity to experience the pleasures of light, open space, green areas, or, even more importantly, decent air to breathe? Or are we continuing to make this same mistakes with respect to these things that we have made in the past? Unfortunately, the evidence seems to indicate that where we don't have planning, and in some of our floundering approaches to planning, we are missing a golden opportunity to improve our environment and the quality of the places in which we live. One gets the impression, in fact, that in many cases we are not only repeating these mistakes but are compounding them in our haste to pursue economic gain.

This is not to take away from the admirable efforts that have been made in some quarters or to deny that we have perhaps prevented the situation from being worse than it is. I find it hard to believe, however, that we have done the best that we can do. One needs only to drive some of our major land-service highways with a sense of awareness to realize that all of that despicable highway clutter was not built before the advent of supposedly advanced thinking in planning and zoning. We still accept the preposterous notion that the ownership of highway frontage endows an individual with the right to capitalize on every possible opportunity of economic self-betterment at the expense of the public. We still permit entrepreneurs and developers, in their anxiety to build hot dog stands, gas stations (even with an energy shortage), fast food outlets, discount marts, and ill-conceived shopping centers, to assure us that no one is willing to live next to a highway and that the idea of open space or green areas went out with the horse and buggy. Yet for years some of the most sought after residential sites have been those with reverse frontage along highways such as the Merritt Parkway in Connecticut and the Garden State Parkway in New Jersey. Nor is this exploitation confined to our highways. An examination of our cities will show that, while more and more of us are talking about the importance of planning and zoning, some of the politicians still ignore plans, making destructive zoning changes under the guise of increasing tax ratables and granting zoning variances that eat the very heart out of the principles of planning and zoning.

THE LAND OF PLENTY—WITH SO MUCH NEED

Why is this so? Why have we failed to get the most out of the planning process and do as well as such other countries as Great Britian, Sweden, and Norway in building new towns and getting the most out of our existing cities? We have more of everything—more land, more cars, more money, more schools, more television, and more chances for advancing our society—but by all standards of quality and sensibility we seem to be determined to fail. I suggest that there may be four basic reasons for this. The first, and probably the most fundamental, is the existence of widespread apathy based upon a frighteningly materialistic attitude. We have been "Madison Avenue'd" to the point that ideals and principles have become entirely secondary to things, goods, products, and a theoretically rising standard of living. This has resulted in an unconcern on the part of the general public toward supporting sound principles of objective planning. It can be summed up by the rather callous attitude, not often openly expressed, that seems to prevail in a lot of us: "I don't care what you do to my town or how much you put in your pocket as long as I get mine."

The second reason for our failure is the fact that our society lacks almost totally a clear concept of the meaning of good planning and zoning. It might even be said that we have no clear concept of what a really good city should be for our day and age. We certainly haven't seen many, and it is, therefore, hard to picture what good planning could do for us. Try, for example, running a little survey of your own. Stop 10 people on the street and ask them to describe city planning for you. If you can get any of them even to attempt it, which is doubtful, you will get as many different opinions as there are people who respond. (As a matter of fact, I still have trouble when people ask me what I "do." When I say I am a planner, the usual response is, "Oh, that's nice. What do you plant?") Our people are not informed on the subject and thus cannot be expected to have a concept. The general public is unaware of any objective standard by which to judge results. People put up with poor planning because they are told it is good and they have no way of knowing otherwise.

Thirdly, and as a corollary, we are suffering from an undisciplined approach to the techniques of planning. If one wishes to be a doctor, lawyer, or scientist, one pursues a reasonably standard course of study, exercising much the same organized perseverence regardless of the school one chooses. In many instances, one then submits to examination, obtains a license, procures a registration, or establishes oneself in a profession. Not so in planning. Anybody can be an expert (even the author of this book), and anybody who has read an article on the subject of planning or held up his or her hand to be sworn in on a planning board can develop the expert complex. As a result, the function of planning suffers, and so do our communities.

Finally, as is true in so many other areas of our complicated social structure, we are suffering from a lack of aggressive, imaginative, and inspiring leadership. This ties in with the first of these reasons for our planning difficulties. When people are unconcerned, when affairs of government are left to others, when business leaders live in the suburbs to escape city problems, when financial forces are little interested in the true economic health of the community that is essentially their life-blood, we will have lackeys and hacks in positions of importance and lackluster leadership will prevail.

THERE IS NO SUCH THING AS THE "RIGHT" OF EXPLOITATION

If these things are true, and if things are not as rosy as they should be, perhaps we should ask ourselves if it isn't time for more effective action. I believe that the argument for the desirability of conserving and, yes, even saving our American cities can be, and should be, one of the most convincing arguments of our times. I am equally convinced that we cannot save our cities without effective planning and zoning. Our past has proved that we need organized planning, to improve conditions for societal living and for mankind, even though it carries with it restriction and regulation. It has been said that people are no more inconsiderate than in their dealings with their neighbors when it comes to land utilization. If this is true—and a poorly planned city is the best possible evidence—it is certainly unfortunate. To ignore the fact that cities can be improved through the development of an orderly sense of purpose and objective is to admit that we cannot learn and instead are doomed to ultimate stagnation by our obstinate unwillingness to change or improve.

We need effective planning to make better economic sense out of our cities and our country. Land and its resources are our most important assets, and the wise utilization of them our greatest opportunity for continuing a sound economy. Exploitation and the misuse of land can result in dire economic consequences for us all. Where, in all of our history and legal precepts, has it been said that a system of public subsidy for personal enrichment—for those clever enough to take full advantage of the opportunity—is the system sanctioned, made sacred, and not to be questioned in a democratic society? Where can it be found in constitutions, laws, or precedents that a collective group of people as a society must accept placidly the idea that resources and land, regardless of ownership, carry with them the right of speculation and wealth, notwithstanding the effect such "rights" may have upon genuine public interest? Yet so we are led to believe by the "growth-is-progress" spellbinders and those who have taken successfully from the land and never given.

Planning is necessary for the sheer survival of our society in the form that we deem desirable. This never was more true than it is today, in the face of the energy crisis, rampant pollution, a shortage of water in many places, and the social crisis in cities. Improved communities, housing conditions, recreational areas, and other aspects of workable city structure are essential to our mental as well as to our economic health. We cannot go on destroying our natural resources, obliterating our landscapes, or planting our fields with 2 by 4 crackerboxes called houses in a dreary, discouraging atmosphere and expect to maintain any kind of a sound social structure.

All of us, then, must recognize that we have a moral responsibility in a complex society to do our best to improve our environment. In accepting this responsibility we must exert an effort to support the causes that will permit us collectively to achieve this improvement. Planning for our cities, towns, and villages is one of the ways in which the environment can be improved and our responsibility met. If our communities are not to be bankrupted by wasteful and uncoordinated development, we must have practical plans for the future. If we are not to be overwhelmed by man-made ugliness, we must see to it that our plans work.

2. The Development of Planning

Whether we realize it or not, governmental planning is all around us; some aspects of our day-to-day lives are being planned or, perhaps, programmed. In our complex social structure, this is necessary and even desirable if we are to preserve our resources and assets and avoid ever greater chaos in the future. The real question we should be asking ourselves, then, is not whether planning is being done but rather whether we are a part of it and are sure that it is the most desirable and the best planning that can be done. This we will never know unless we are involved as citizens. If we get involved, we will find that today's concept of planning is quite different from that of the past—and that the change is very much for the better.

Planning as a process has progressed from the largely theoretical and frequently impractical ivory-tower approach to today's deliberate, hardheaded analysis of all aspects of city, community, and regional problems, whether they be physical, social, or economic. No longer is the planner concerned merely with the physical design or growth of a given area. Now he or she deals with the sometimes staggering facts of housing needs, social programs, downtown rebuilding, parks and open space, schools, sewers, employment potentials, street and road improvements—all of the municipal needs and facilities that must be supported by taxes and that hit the taxpayers where they feel it most: in their pocketbooks. Today any municipality in any state can organize a planning program as a governmental function. Your community may have already done so. Not only do state statutes allow municipalities to engage in planning activities, but in most states planning is encouraged at county and regional levels. Careful procedures are established by legislation setting forth the type of organization that is necessary. We should be familiar with these, as well as with the work of all planning agencies that may have any bearing on our lives, so that we can judge factually and have a voice in the deliberations.

THE EVOLUTION OF THE PROCESS

While no attempt will be made in this book to explore thoroughly all of the influences of the past and the complete historic evolution of communities and urban form, a quick review of a few of the major milestones is important to an understanding of today's problems and current planning endeavors. Cities have been "planned" to one extent or another for almost as long as they have been built. Even the earliest prehistoric villages and ancient cities had preconceived form as well as controls designed to achieve that form. From the earliest time of the grouping together of people into communities, there have been fundamental reasons for cities other than what may be described as an inherent need for societal living. These reasons have included dictates and desires of rulers, protection, availability of resources, culture, education, commerce, trade, and economic betterment. In order to respond to these various requisites, cities were located in particular places because of the topography, climate, available water, or tactical advantages that made communal living possible, desirable, or sensible. Bodies of water, the confluence of rivers, and river valleys, for example, became the points of origination for many cities.

Many features of these early cities carried over into our cities today, and we have learned much from the city builders and "planners" of Egypt, Greece, Italy, France, Sweden, and Great Britain. The major milestones that have affected American city form and planning up to the 20th century, however, are chiefly these:

1. The rectilinear (gridiron) city plan credited to Hippodamus of Miletus in the 5th century BC.

2. The invention and spread of gunpowder, beginning in the early 14th century, which made the walled city obsolete and resulted in the spreading out of the urban form.

3. The Renaissance Baroque design form, which gave flexibility to the designer for free-flowing and open city planning.

4. The Industrial Revolution and its technological developments, which changed life-styles and ideas of a standard of living.

5. Colonialism, with its resulting development of commerce and trade and the formation of new settlements and cities.

6. Frontierism and western expansion in the U.S.

7. The English Garden City movement, bringing with it an appreciation of a degree of open space and green living environment.

8. The 1893 World's Columbian Exposition in Chicago and the birth of a Neoclassic design style in the U.S.

When one reflects on the cities in which we live today, it is easy to see the influences over the years of these events or eras. It is also easy to see that none of the above, founded in the technology of their times, anticipated the monstrous effect of the internal-combustion engine and the automobile. Thus, one of our major planning problems, especially with older cities, lies in trying to adapt long-established urban physical structure to 20th- and 21st-century living patterns.

To most people, the start of modern-day city planning is considered to be the 1893 World's Columbian Exposition in Chicago. While it is true that plans for development for many of our cities had been prepared prior to 1893, the attempt made in Chicago to breathe a bit of aesthetics and social consciousness into urban life was strongly felt during the 36 years that followed the Exposition and preceded the 1929 stock market crash. Some of the best known earlier plans that should be noted are those for Williamsburg, Virginia (settled in 1633); Philadelphia (1682); Savannah, Georgia (1733); Washington, D.C. (1791); Buffalo, New York (1804); and Detroit (1807). The New York City Commission Plan of 1811 should be included as well. As we view these cities today, it is easy to be overly critical of the lack of foresight and the dominance of economic consideration over physical and social amenities.

While many of these plans were lacking in concern for people, especially future generations, nowhere is criticism seemingly more justified than in analyzing the inherited plight of New York City. After rejecting a previous plan by Joseph Mangin, an architect and surveyor, the designated commission was led by the pressures of exploitive interests and economic gain for a few simply to superimpose on Manhattan Island the unimaginative and uninspiring plan we see today.

In their book *The Urban Pattern* (1975), Arthur B. Gallion and Simon Eisner sum it up well:

> The position of the commission was quite clear: "Straight-sided and right-angled houses," they reported, "are the most cheap to build and the most convenient to live in." The matter of economy obviously guided the commission in its deliberations and dictated its conclusions. They found that "the price of land is so uncommonly great" and their proposal for retention of open space was indeed frugal. . . . [It was not until 1856 that the city acquired the land for Central Park at a cost to the citizens of $5,500,000 for the 800 acres.] But it is the economy of the commission that poses the most pertinent issue because it bears strong resemblance to that practiced in later and less happy days of urban planning. . . . The commission surely expected the city to continue the growth it was then enjoying: they obviously did for they so mapped it for subdivision and sale. . . . This is the variety of economy that distorts the planning of our cities today. . . . There were those who protested the formlessness of the commissioner's plan. Many agreed with Henry R. Aldrich when he claimed its inspiration was "the great facility which it provides for the gambling in land values and ready purchase and sale of building blocks" which had "wrought incalculable mischief." It was an omen of the fate to befall the American city in subsequent years.

WHERE THERE IS MUCK, YOU CAN ALWAYS FIND A RAKE

By 1893 the results of such shortsightedness and greed could be clearly seen, not only in New York City but also in many other cities. Tenement houses, slums, filth, and disparaging conditions were rampant. A few socially conscious journalists such as Lincoln Steffens, then referred to as "muckrakers," had begun to call the public's attention to these ills. The stage was set for a reaction. This took the form of the "White City," or as it was to become known, the "City Beautiful," which was the theme of the Chicago Exposition of that year. Beautiful white facades, dazzling esplanades, and bubbling fountains offered urban dwellers some escape from what our cities had become and, at the same time, served to inspire many visitors to return home and try to do something about "beautifying" their own drab urban environment. In his book *American City Planning* (1969), Mel Scott says:

> ...the brilliant image of symmetrical edifices, colossal statues, and stupendous domes burned in memory long after the summer pilgrims had returned to their lackluster commercial cities, dreary mill towns, and homely prairie villages. Plastic fantasy that it was, the World's Columbian Exposition touched the deep longing of a nation suffering from a loss of continuity with history for visual assurance of maturity and success. Not the creative and office blocks in downtown Chicago, but the specious classicism of the fair satisfied the hunger for cultural security and self-approbation.

Thus was born the "City Beautiful" movement and, in effect, the basis of the theory that urban form, if left to individual motivations, might not be always the best and that the viability of the city was a matter of public as well as private concern. Following the turn of the century, many local communities undertook "city beautifying" projects. Civic centers, public plazas, and massive monumental structures in classical styles were advocated, initiated, and accomplished by governments, civic leaders, and citizen groups—all, unfortunately, showing little regard for the social and economic problems of the people. Nevertheless, the igniting of the spark of human concern and sense of the interrelation of social and economic factors to physical form was achieved, and the flame slowly spread.

While cities had begun to utilize the "police power" inherent in government in regulating land use (primarily this took the form of restrictions against use of a nuisance variety), it was not until 1916 that zoning was shaped into the form in which we know it today. In the meantime, the word "planning" began to be bandied about more and more as a governmental function. Cities recognized the need for a sense of direction, a comprehensive overview of where they were and where they were heading. Daniel Burnham, one of the principal architects of the Chicago Exposition, was asked to develop a plan for the lakefront, which grew into a plan for the entire Chicago region. In 1907, Hartford, Connecticut, became the first city to establish an official planning commission and was quickly followed by Milwaukee (1908) and Chicago (1909). In 1909 the First National Conference on City Planning was held in Washington. Also in 1909, Wisconsin enacted a state-enabling act authorizing cities of the second and third class to create planning commissions. The State of Massachusetts, in 1913, went further by requiring all cities over 10,000 in population to have planning commissions.

ZONING AND INCREASED GOVERNMENTAL ACTION

As planning efforts on the part of governments grew, the realization also grew that the advisory nature of plans needed methods and tools of enforcement. Early efforts at land use regulation were put into a comprehensive zoning ordinance in New York City in 1916. Here was the first attempt to combine, in one police-power ordinance, restrictions on and regulations for land use, height and bulk of buildings, and the density of population and development. Much of the credit for this work is given to Frank M. Bassett, a prominent New York lawyer in his time. Following this action, cities all over the country began to climb on the zoning bandwagon. (For further discussion, see "Chapter 6. The Relationship of Zoning to Planning.")

Progress was interrupted by the outbreak of World War I, but with its end and the resumption of the pursuit of the great American dream, growth of cities again received attention. Zoning became more popular; but as there was little for guidance other than the New York City ordinance and some state enabling acts, which varied greatly, a federal agency undertook to provide some degree of standardization. The United States Department of Commerce, under Secretary Herbert Hoover, in 1922 developed "A Standard State Zoning Enabling Act." While there have been many changes in our concerns, problems, and approaches since then, the language of this model will still be found in the enabling legislation of most states pertaining to zoning. It might also be noted at this point that, although zoning is now firmly established as a tool of planning to be *preceded* by comprehensive planning studies, the mood of the country—and the resulting federal action—actually placed the zoning cart before the horse of land planning. It was not until 1928 that this fact was officially recognized and the Department of Commerce promulgated "A Standard State Planning Enabling Act."

Following the crash of the stock market in 1929, every state and federal agency became involved in dealing with the Depression and restoring the economy. As private construction came to a virtual halt, public works planning and projects became the thing of the hour. Using the model acts as format, many states adopted planning legislation, and by 1936 almost all states had created state planning boards. These agencies not only busied themselves with proposals for public facilities but also did excellent work in areas of statewide land use, natural resources inventory, transportation projects, and public open-space preservation. This was the time of the beginning of the "alphabet soup" of federal aid programs such as the NRA, RFC, WPA, and PWA. It was correspondingly the time of increased emphasis on the need for the elements of the planning process and the realization that the shape of the future of our urban areas and our environment is a public responsibility.

By 1936 the war clouds were gathering again, and the country once more turned its attention to military matters. In passing, we can note the start of the first low-rent housing programs through the enactment of the Public Housing Act of 1937. This was to be a milestone on the road the federal government was to travel in broadening public responsibility for social needs and in setting the stage for the increased involvement of Washington in matters long thought of as local problems. This recognition of housing needs for all income levels led to an increased demand for greater advance planning.

It was during the Depression period that we were given a telling object lesson regarding the difficulty of having sensible, organized planning in our political system and profit-oriented economy. In 1939, through pressure from some concerned citizens and President Franklin D. Roosevelt, the National Resources Planning Board (NRPB) was created. Probably one of the most logical and sensible things ever done by the federal government, its purpose was not only to examine resources availability but also to assure coordination of federal programs and develop national policies to guide future growth and development. While the NRPB accomplished many things during its existence, including the stimulation of considerable state planning activity, its objective view of the utilization of resources and allocation of public works and monies unfortunately left something to be desired from the viewpoint of Congress and the bureaucracy. As a result, under pressure from certain Congressional members, the NRPB was abolished in 1943, leaving the Congressional committees with free rein to continue pork-barrelling. Once again the national defense theme and the military buildup became the principal concerns of the country, unfettered by any resource or environmental considerations.

Following World War II, from the standpoint of community development and urban form, all hell broke loose. With an exploding birth rate and the return of the military to civilian life, some areas began to look as if we were intent upon creating wall-to-wall urbanism. Aided and abetted by the Federal Housing Administration's policy of easy mortgage money for new houses in suburbia, the years between 1946 and 1954 became the speculative developer's paradise. While there was a rush to push through more zoning ordinances and to revise some of the older ones, local governments could not keep up with, much less stay ahead of, the bulldozer. Municipalities and municipal service systems, as well as educational systems, were literally overrun. Building starts appeared like mushrooms; peach orchards, cornfields, and even swamps sprouted what was to become the symbol of the great American dream—the ticky-tacky house in an even more ticky-tacky subdivision.

Albuquerque, New Mexico, is a good example of what was happening nationwide. In 1940 it was a sleepy dusty town of 55,000. By 1950 it had grown to 95,000 as a result of the federal government's having discovered New Mexico and established such things as Los Alamos, Kirtland Air Force Base, and Sandia Base. Left unbridled and largely undirected, this growth continued until by 1960 Albuquerque was a "city" of 210,000 in a metropolitan area of 262,000 people. Here and elsewhere, after the bulldozers and construction crews left, came the dawn of realism from overflowing septic tanks, contaminated water supplies, crises in traffic congestion, and double and triple school sessions. Communities rushed frantically to create planning boards, adopt subdivision ordinances, set up building codes, insert minimum dwelling size requirements in zoning ordinances, and generally apply bandages to gaping wounds.

While some sound planning was done during this period and those places that had had the foresight to establish and staff a planning process in advance fared reasonably well, most of the efforts to deal with the problems proved to be futile or inadequate crisis reaction rather than positive advance planning. Some of this resulted from the specific unavailability of local-level funding for planning and professional services and some from the lack of recognition of the importance of and knowledge about effective municipal planning. For whatever reason, a serious problem of national significance had arisen, with a resulting void in solution ability at the local level. Invariably, when this occurs, a higher level of government is going to be called on or is only too ready to volunteer to fill the void. In this case the federal government attempted to do so.

THE 1954 FEDERAL HOUSING ACT: "THE CARROT AND BIG STICK"

Probably the biggest turning point in spreading local planning activity and, for better or worse, shaping the format of the elements of a planning process was the Federal Housing Act of 1954. Through urban redevelopment legislation since 1946, cities had been aided by federal funds to acquire and clear slums and make the cleared land available for residential re-use. The 1954 act went much further, causing municipal planning activity to take a giant step forward in numbers, if not in effectiveness. The impetus was provided by two sections of the act that (1) established a mandatory requirement for comprehensive planning as a prerequisite to funding for urban renewal and (2) put the federal government in the business of providing financial aid for municipal, county, regional, and eventually even state planning.

Under the terms of this legislation, any city that wanted to undertake urban renewal was required to develop a "workable program for community improvement" (WPCI). The first of seven elements to be included was a comprehensive master plan, or at least significant progress toward that end; otherwise no further federal assistance would be forthcoming. The legislation's other major feature was the reasonably short Section 701, which led to what became known as the "701 Program." This section recognized the need for planning in general at the community level as well as the fact that the mandatory requirement for planning would call for the expenditure of funds that some communities would be hard pressed to find. Consequently, it provided for a system of funding master plan studies through approved state agencies. At first only for communities under 25,000 in population on a fifty-fifty funding basis, this was later changed to allow larger municipalities and regions to participate. The local-share requirement was reduced to 25 percent of the costs. Needless to say, the "big stick" requirement of a master plan in order to qualify for other federal funds and the "carrot dangling" of financial aid brought about over a thousand master plan studies and added greatly to the number of organized planning programs. (The consulting firm I headed prepared over 300 of these "701 Program" plans for municipalities, counties, and regions in the eastern coastal area in the period from 1954 to 1970; and we were not alone in this kind of activity.)

There has been much debate about the "701 Program" and its effectiveness. Did it really result in a vast array of well-structured plans that in turn helped to make cities better places, or was it just a prime example of local-federal game playing and a waste of tax money? Can we say that the planning studies resulted in action to avoid mistakes or to correct ones already made? Were there situations in which communities entered the program and arranged to have plans prepared only because they labored under the illusion that they ought to take advantage of that "free" federal money?

Let it suffice to say that, while there was both good and bad planning done, the program accomplished at least two things. First, it served as a means of firmly defining a role of interest, even if somewhat proprietary and regulative, of the federal government in local community development. To some, this meant an encouragement of direct relations between cities and the federal system and a by-pass of state jurisdiction and prerogative. To others, even if this were the case, this was a necessary and beneficial move because states had failed to act or had been unable to cope. There are those who feel that the blame for many, if not most, of our urban ills can be placed squarely at the feet of insensitive, ineffectual, unconcerned, and inept state legislatures. States, on the other hand, are quick to respond that the federal government has usurped the primary sources of revenue and that the solution lies where the money is.

Second, the Federal Housing Act of 1954 gave a new emphasis to local planning that served to create planning consciousness throughout the country. Even if the planning accomplished did not happen to be the best, the fact that it was going on caused many more to hear about it, become involved, and learn something about the problems of keeping a municipal government's house in order. Perhaps for this reason alone, the "701 Program" has been worth the money and the effort. Since the inception of the program to aid local planning, there have been many changes in its requirements and new approaches added to the federal-aid market basket. Today, the program still provides money for large metropolitan area planning and for regional planning and, through the latter, some assistance for local planning.

Washington's attempts to encourage local action have continued at a steady pace, including the creation of the Department of Housing and Urban Development (HUD) in 1965 as well as the promulgation of such laws and programs as the Demonstration Cities and Metropolitan Development Act ("Model Cities" program) in 1966; the New Communities Act ("New Towns") of 1968; Secretary George Romney's "Operation Breakthrough" housing program in 1969; and the Urban Growth and Community Development Act of 1970, which included sections designed to assist the development of "New Towns-In Town" to encourage large-scale rebuilding of older cities.

THE "NEW FEDERALISM" AND REVENUE SHARING

With the Nixon administration and its "New Federalism," the emphasis shifted from "categorical" (by specific function) funding to the philosophy of allocating money to the cities and allowing them, under certain restrictions and guidelines, to determine priorities for spending it. A city more seriously concerned about social programs than about streets and sewer plants could, for example, decide to concentrate in social program areas. Based upon the "let the local people decide" theme, general revenue sharing was born.

I still remember the day a city of which I was city manager received its first revenue sharing check for over $5 million. At the time, we all thought that the millennium had arrived; little did we know the headaches that were to come later in deciding how to spend the money and what was to happen to categorical funding. From there we have gone to a modification of the Nixon proposal for special, or block grant, revenue sharing. In 1974, the Housing and Community Development Act was passed. This legislation, supported by organizations representing the interests of the cities, consolidated various categorically funded programs of HUD into a single block or package grant system. This meant that there would no longer be separate programs for urban renewal, model cities, neighborhood facilities, open-space land, or basic water and sewer facilities. Instead, Community Development Act funds would be provided to each city, as well as to the states, based upon a formula designed to attempt to assure "fair and equitable" distribution. The allocation would be left to local option. As had been true in recent years, the federal government insisted that there be citizen involvement in determination of how the funds would be spent. While this program will be subject to change with changing administrations and personnel, it is the method in use at the moment for aiding and encouraging the major elements within community development related to planning.

So we have come full circle from the days of indiscriminate use of resources, permitting cities just to happen, and encouraging suburban sprawl with little or no restrictions to present-day community, county, regional, and state planning with necessary standards and regulations—all accepted as logical and essential functions of government. Regardless of where we live, in all probability we fall under the purview of a planning agency. What they are doing with our most precious assets, land, and resources, as well as what they are doing that may have a bearing on the quality and character of where we live, work, and have our economic and social future, is something that should concern us all. Where we go from here and whether the things that are done through planning or under the guise of planning will be any good and make our future cities, our communities, and our rural areas better places is largely up to us as citizens.

I tell my students that no planning will be successful unless there is a planning attitude within the affected area on the part of citizens, political leaders, and the power structure. Where this is not so, what is called planning can be an illusory gimmick used to develop a false sense of security on the part of those of us who are prone to apathy concerning local government and our community. Today, more than ever before, sensible, organized citizen concern can be heard and can be effective. Long-range and comprehensive local planning, not just short-run problemsolving, is the citizen's greatest hope for assuring that which is best for all of us as well as the community of the future, whether it be a physical, social, or economic concern. I suggest also that community planning with meaningful citizen involvement is one of the last ways available to us in trying to preserve a true democratic society.

3. The Planning Process

When you hear the word "planning," what image is created in your mind? Do you think of architecture, buildings, sewer lines, streets, and other things relating to physical aspects of development? Perhaps the term connotes concern over environmental factors like air quality control, preservation of open space, conservation of resources, and regulation of nuclear power plants. Those of us interested in some of the social problems of society immediately conjure up ideas of housing programs, welfare improvement, equal employment opportunities, medical and senior citizen care, and a myriad of other things. If you are in industry or business, planning means research and development of new products, new plant construction, expansion of operation within financial capabilities, meeting competition, and determination of present and future market potentials. On the other hand, to a great number of people, the term is extremely negative and brings forth nothing but images of governmental control, the intrusion of Big Brother into private lives and private rights, and a "planned economy." "After all," these latter say, "we certainly don't want any of that kind of stuff, because isn't that what they have in those Communistic countries?"

Just a week before writing this, I was in a small Colorado town where this attitude continues to be very prevalent. Yet I was there because they wanted advice on how to deal with a situation in which they faced a hodgepodge land-use pattern, had lost their one major industry, possessed a water system inadequate to serve their people, and had been ordered by the Environmental Protection Agency and the state health department to do something about the open lagoons they had been using for sewage treatment. Still, they feel that people and government working together in organized planning is Communistic and something to be avoided at all cost.

PLANNING'S ROLE IN TODAY'S SOCIETY

We can see from this that one of the great difficulties in applying the term "planning" to a governmental function is the lack of understanding of the proper role and an absence of a common concept as to the meaning of the word. We accept the fact that there is practically nothing that goes on in our private lives and our economy-oriented society that, if we are orderly people or shrewd investors, should not be well thought out and planned ahead. But when it comes to organizing our total environment and community development, from either a lack of information, a lack of interest, or some personal hang-up, we object to or end up in confusion over what should be done.

This is not totally the fault of us as individuals. Part of the problem lies in the history of our country and its development policies, part in a failure of the planning profession, and part in the practices of the past in politics and in the "politics" of planning. Since the founding of our federation of states, we have enjoyed the privilege of a freewheeling, frontier-type expansion and growth. The idea existed that resources were inexhaustible, that land was unlimited, and it was every person's right to do as he or she damn well pleased as long as that could not be shown to be directly and overtly harmful to someone else. Governmental policies encouraged this through homesteading acts, support and subsidization of the railroads for development expansion, FHA single-family-home mortgaging, and general deifying of the philosophy that there is a pot of gold at the end of every rainbow for everybody. After all, aren't we one of the largest, richest, and most well-endowed nations in the world, founded on the principles of freedom, individual liberty, and justice for all? Why worry about the future in terms of city building, farmland protection, and environment when we have all those good things going for us?

It is this concept that, while generally sound and admirable, has had to be adjusted somewhat to changing conditions throughout our 200-year history. Many of us find this adjustment hard to make and painful to accept. There are others who have not accepted, and probably never will, the inescapable truth that the sheer survival of society, of us all, depends upon our being able to change our thinking and our approach to societal living in a reasonable way. Instead, oblivious to the facts, they hang on unswervingly to the notion that such adjustment is against the principles of democracy and that what they consider to be private "rights" must be forever sacrosanct. For better or worse, we must begin to recognize we cannot retain a frontier mentality in an ever-expanding, socially complex 21st-century world. This is, and will continue to be, something with which we all must learn to deal and to live.

I KNOW YOU UNDERSTAND WHAT YOU THINK I SAID, BUT I AM NOT SURE YOU REALIZE THAT WHAT YOU HEARD IS NOT WHAT I MEANT

From the planning profession's standpoint, I am afraid we have failed in a number of ways. First of all, even after more than a half-century of organized community planning, those involved in education, practice, and effectuation have not arrived at an agreed-upon definition of the term—or of the planner's responsibility—so that planning can be clearly understood and seen as a necessity by the general public. We planners talk about such things as demography, cohorts, regression theory, computer modeling, projections, input-output studies, etc., that become relatively meaningless and unimpressive to anyone largely concerned with property values and taxes. While the need for putting it all together for any community or city is there, and is becoming more and more obvious, we planners have yet to develop a common professional framework that lets the public know that the process in which we believe is something upon which they can and should rely.

This leads into the second shortcoming of the profession: planners have done an inadequate job of telling the community-planning story to the populace. One of the major reasons for the variety of conceptual ideas and some of the misconceptions about planning is the fact that no unified voice has been heard sounding the reasons for good planning, explaining it in lay terms, and, without being only a harbinger of doom and gloom, pointing out the pitfalls and dangers of leaving the future to chance. After being a member of the American Institute of Planners (AIP) for over 25 years, I can say it has always been my hope that AIP might provide that unified voice; but, alas, I may not live long enough to see that come to pass.

Thirdly, we have the politics, or lack thereof, in planning. I have chosen that phrase purposely, even though there are many who will say that is what is wrong with planning now—there is too much politics involved. But is there too much or not enough? Have we perhaps labored too long under the illusion that planning per se should be entirely free of political stigma and, as a consequence, permitted the professional politician to turn planning off and on like a water faucet, conveniently using or not using it to suit the purpose of the moment? I have little patience with those who use the shotgun approach of blaming "those planners" for failing to improve America's cities. The very nature of the process has been that those skilled in community planning recommend and policymakers (politicians?) effectuate.

In reality, the albatross that planners have permitted to be hung around their necks—the blame for a plethora of planning studies and reports that only ended up on a shelf gathering dust—is misplaced. It should be loudly and ceremoniously hung around the necks of those who, from either self-interest, response to pressure, or lack of guts, have found it served their purposes best not to rock the boat with long-range or comprehensive problems and ideas. In many cases, because of such equivocators, the professional planner has become a scapegoat and, not being able to speak openly against his or her political bosses, has been hung for doing an unworkable plan. Unfortunately, this state of affairs has been fostered by a number of newspaper reporters and other writers who have found it easy and convenient, for their purposes, to lay the responsibility for all planning actions—or the failed actions of elected officials, federal agencies, architects, developers, and bankers—at the feet of "those planners," thus adding to the public's misconception of the profession. Outstanding examples of this are Jane Jacobs in her *Death and Life of Great American Cities* (1961), Robert Goodman's *After the Planners* (1972), and the general writings of Herbert J. Gans, particularly *The Levittowners* (1967).

Be that as it may, the need for community planning and the understanding of it by citizens continues to grow. It is my belief that understanding must be based on knowledge, and, although it may seem elementary, a definition of terms is always helpful. One of those given for the word "plan" by *Webster's New World Dictionary* is, "a scheme or program for making, doing, or arranging something; project, design, schedule, etc." What we are talking about, therefore, in the community planning process is the community working together to develop a scheme or program for doing that which makes the most sense and is the best approach for communal living for everybody. This doesn't mean simply that the planners plan and the politicians and citizens sit back in judgment. It means that the professionals provide information, the people express desires and needs (and, in effect, plan), and those elected to serve carry out the scheme. This is a good opportunity to reiterate the statement made previously that a planning attitude must permeate the community, or at least the "shakers and movers," for any planning to succeed. The most successful planners have been those who not only were able to instill this in the minds of the people in their areas of jurisdiction but also took an active role in seeing that "right-thinking" people were elected.

DEFINING THE PLANNING PROCESS

Like everything else having to do with urban growth, the problems of cities, and what is happening to rural America, there has been a great deal written about the planning process. It may help our understanding if we look at some other attempts at definition. In the bible of planning education—lovingly referred to by students as "the Jolly Green Giant" due to its size and color, but more formally known as *Principles and Practice of Urban Planning* (1968)—the editors have, unfortunately, omitted a description of the planning function that appeared in an earlier edition of the book called *Local Planning Administration* (1959). While it may be a bit dated, I think it worth repeating here:

> The broad object of planning is to further the welfare of the people in the community by helping to create an increasingly better, more healthful, convenient, efficient and attractive community environment. The physical, as well as the social and economic community is a single organism, all features and activities of which are related and interdependent. These facts must be supplemented by the application of intelligent foresight and planned administrative and legal coordination if balance, harmony and order are to be insured. It is the task of planning to supply this foresight and this over-all coordination.

It has been previously indicated that the federal government is heavily involved in all levels of planning through its system of financial aid. As is always the case, if federal dollars come, following not far behind will be federal "guidelines," standards, restrictions, and definitions. In stating the purpose of federal planning assistance programs, the "Catalog of Federal Aids to State and Local Governments" provides the following:

> Comprehensive planning is defined as including, to the extent directly related to urban needs, the preparation of general physical plans for land use and the provision of public facilities (including transportation facilities), with long-range fiscal plans to accompany the long-range development plans; the programing of capital improvements and their financing; coordination of all related plans of the departments and subdivisions of the government concerned; intergovernmental coordination of planning activities; and the preparation of supporting regulatory and administrative measures.

A much more simple statement—and one probably more effective and meaningful than the above bureaucratese—can be found in Thomas F. Saarinen's *Environmental Planning: Perception and Behavior* (1976):

> Planning may be considered the conscious organization of human activities to serve human needs. Better planning can be accomplished by greater integration of the separate components at each scale into a broader, more coherent framework. To be effective, planning must consider not only the physical environment but the way people perceive and utilize each segment of the environment.

Dr. Joel B. Goldsteen, director of the city and regional planning program at the University of Texas at Arlington carries this on further by saying that he likes to think of planning as "the end product of environmental controls on the physical city or region and the shaping of all the social, economic and political variables affecting that end product."

We could go on with any number of other definitions, but I believe a sufficient basis has been laid for the understanding of the process and of what planning can and should do. Although the term can be applied appropriately to any activity, the thing that we as citizens should be able to be discriminate about it is that it refers specifically to the application of intelligent foresight to the future of our community and its character and of our environment.

NOW, LET'S PUT HUMPTY DUMPTY TOGETHER

The basis for all planning activity is the proper delegation of governmental administrative responsibility and authority. This starts with the enabling legislation adopted by the state, allowing county and municipal governments to organize for planning. All of us should be familiar with this legislation as the wording of the act sets the pattern for what can and cannot be done, even for home-rule cities. From this point we move to the local scene. To get started in planning, the governing body must enact an ordinance establishing an agency for planning (a planning commission or planning board, depending upon the terminology of each state act) and setting forth its prescribed functions. Once this has been done, there are the questions of appointments to the commission, the possible need for professional staff to do the work, and the structuring of the function into the local government. For more discussion of the makeup of the commission, its role, etc., see "Chapter 4. The Planning Commission."

Traditionally, the first major task assigned to the planning commission has been the preparation of a master plan for the entire area of its jurisdiction. Equally traditional has been the fact that the formulation of a plan is based upon an existing conditions inventory or a "resources analysis," the purpose of the plan being to allocate resources to meet best the needs of the total community. In recent years there have been those who have faulted this approach in support of a more grass-roots type of procedure. The argument has been toward first determining goals and objectives through greater citizen involvement by neighborhoods and citizen action groups. Objectives should be based upon the desires of the people and the available resources, adjusted to see that these wants and desires are given priority.

John Friedmann is one of those who has been most outspoken against the traditional style of planning. In his book *Retracking America* (1973) he points out what he considers to be the faults of "allocative" planning, which he defines as "the distribution of limited resources among a number of competing users." He proposes that the process be changed to "innovative planning," which he says "is largely a self-executing activity; the formulation and carrying out of plans constitute, in this case, a single operation." In general it seems that Friedmann's thesis is that planning, to be effective, must involve more participation of competing interest groups in policy determination and that this may require institutional change rather than just central re-allocation of resources. One of his reasons for concern over allocative practices is that complex modern society is dominated by special interest groups that have sufficient power to frustrate the intentions of any plan that threatens their interest. As he puts it, "allocative planning serves primarily the interests of those who are already strong." From my experience as both a planning director and a city manager in a city dominated and controlled by real estate speculators, developers, and commercial exploiters and their assembled clique, I can't argue too enthusiastically against Friedmann's thesis.

Whether Friedmann's proposition is the correct one or not, there has been and continues to be a diversity of opinion and a great amount of discussion on what the proper planning function is and how it should be carried out. There is little debate remaining, at least among the more informed people in any area where urbanization has occurred or is occurring, over whether there should be governmental planning to ensure public benefit. The facts indicate that, with the encouragement of federal requirements and enticements, we are well established in an era of structured planning, even if it is in name only and leaves much to be desired.

The debate will, and should, continue over how and by whom planning should be done. One thing that seems certain, however, is that there will be increased citizen involvement in determining goals and objectives, the formulation of official plans to achieve these objectives, and the means utilized for effectuation. Planning efforts, in turn, must broaden the traditional scope of coverage to include more social concerns. The establishment of priorities for funding programs as compared to projects will become a major issue. In larger urban areas the competition between central planning and neighborhood self-determination is steadfastly on the increase. Whether a community-wide master plan should be assembled from a collection of neighborhood or micro-unit plans or the broader view taken first and neighborhood planning adjusted as part of the whole is one of the first policy decisions that should be made in organization of a planning program. Even if planning has long existed, this is a current dilemma that should be freely and openly discussed if the results are to be successful.

A ROSE BY ANY OTHER NAME

For our purposes in this book, regardless of the divergent opinions as to procedure, it is reasonable to assume that whatever *form* we find most appropriate will nonetheless utilize the available *tools* for planning. Again, although these have undergone and will undergo changes, a view of the future does not indicate that, in our form of governmental system, we will be able to abandon the traditional methods of land-use controls, environmental protection, urban form shaping, and financing of projects and programs. In other words, while the approach to and the format of a master plan may change, there will still be the need for a basic frame of reference to give us a sense of direction. Call it what you will, under our system of law and under statutes that state legislatures will be willing to adopt, a form of "master plan" that will continue to be advisory and recommendatory in nature will be fundamental and the touchstone in the planning process. Whether this is a "policies plan" or a "physical plan" (see "Chapter 5. The Master Plan") is up to each community to determine. In either case, it is important that we as citizens be informed and know just what is meant when someone tells us that something is being done because "it is in accordance with the master plan."

A second tool is zoning (see "Chapter 6. The Relationship of Zoning to Planning"). Even though, as previously stated, zoning came into general acceptance before organized planning, the fact is well established now that, to be properly and effectively done, such land-use controls as zoning should be based upon a well-thought-out comprehensive plan. Whether this occurs in actuality or not, zoning has become an extremely powerful instrument of government. There are few other adopted laws of local government that affect our private lives and our economic well-being more. In meetings with my students, I have frequently asked them the question, "If you had the desire to make yourself into a dictator or totalitarian monarch in the United States, absolute control over what two things would make this the easiest to accomplish?" They usually have little trouble with one of these—offering "the minds of the people" as an excellent possibility. They have put forth a variety of ideas for the second, and they sometimes express shock when I propose the theory that the complete control of the use of land is another excellent choice. Careful analysis will tell you that this is the fundamental base of all economics and that, next to mind manipulation, the most effective weapon for human behavior control is control of individual economic opportunity—the control of the pocketbook. This is why I have difficulty understanding the lack of general concern and interest on the part of the public about zoning.

The power to control land use is one of the most important powers allocated to government. Used properly, it can be one of the greatest assets in improving our communities' character, our environment, and our way of life. Used improperly, it can be a means of political retribution, service to special vested interests, personal economic enrichment, and the attainment of more power. Unfortunately, I have seen it used for all of these purposes in more than one community. A more flagrant case involved a city where the dominant force on a planning commission was a very influential real estate broker who headed one of the city's largest firms. It was amazing how all zoning changes in which he, his firm, or his closest "pals" were involved slipped through so easily while those proposed by or benefiting competing real estate brokers invariably were found to be "contrary to the public interest" and usually rejected. Quite naturally, the commissioner's volume of business did not suffer from this.

How the power to control land use is used depends upon how much we as citizens know about it and how involved we are in making sure that any action taken does result in a benefit to the "public health, safety, and general welfare"—the charge established in all zoning legislation. Zoning, in whatever form may be devised, whether it includes such modern techniques as planned unit developments, growth management programs, or transfer of development rights, will still be a major mechanism for shaping urban and suburban form and the activities in rural areas. As such it only makes sense for each person to fully understand not only the principles and theories of zoning but also the methods of administration and enforcement employed.

In planning circles it has become habitual to point out to anyone who will listen that the only major city in the United States that does not have a zoning ordinance is Houston, Texas. In fact the citizens of Houston have, on several occasions, voted down the very idea. Some years ago, in a speech given at a national planning conference, I heard the then mayor of Houston defend his city's "lack of modern land use controls" by saying that, through his visits to other cities where zoning existed, he failed to find they were any better. They still had hodge-podge development, transportation arteries lined with cheap commercial establishments, and just as much environmental pollution as did his city. While the mayor was correct basically, he could have been saying, in effect, "Our slums are no worse than your slums, and we haven't even let it bother us." Actually, this was not the thrust of his remark, for he went on to point out that much of the same type of land-use controls and development guidance had been achieved, in Houston, by the use of deed restrictions or private land covenants and, even more importantly, through effective subdivision controls—the third basic tool of planning.

In theory, the use of governmental police power to establish standards for the subdivision of land supplements zoning and does not relate to land use, building placement, parking requirements, etc., found in zoning ordinances. Subdivision controls, as Houston has seen, can be a most effective and important means of aiding in the planning process. It is important to understand that, while planning and the master plan are considered advisory, the implementing strength lies in the two uses of the police power right of government to restrict each of us for the public good—zoning and subdivision controls. Both of these must be correlated closely with the master planning process and used only in a way to carry out the objectives of that process. (For further discussion, see "Chapter 7. The Regulation of Land Subdivision.")

The fourth tool of planning about which we should talk in some depth is the capital improvements program. As vital as this is to the establishment of community character, the running of effective government, and the tax demands on each and every one of us, it never ceases to amaze me how little is known about it and how little it concerns most of us. Yet every community has a capital expenditure program, whether planned or not; and it accounts for a large part of the local taxes we pay and is the largest single item, other than schools, deriving its financial support from the real estate property tax—that tidy sum we pay with each mortgage payment or periodically on our homes or whatever real estate we own. Put simply, capital improvement expenditures are the way that all public improvements, be they school facilities, parks, sewers, water lines, libraries, museums, streets, or what have you, are provided, repaired, improved, or enlarged. These are the source of the amenities of a community, the things that make it attractive to developers, industrialists, business persons, and ordinary home owners. Together with the efficiency of administration, a progressive attitude, and meaningful and effective social programs, capital facilities provide the trunk of the tree of intangible aspects that make the difference between a good community and one that just is. They are the spinal cord upon which can be built a healthy community body. Here again, without citizen awareness and involvement, the use and distribution of these funds can be misdirected and made into a powerful political force.

In these days of large amounts of federal aid, fortunately, the allocating agencies are insisting on citizen involvement in the decisionmaking process. Under the Revenue Sharing Act of 1972 and the 1974 Community Development Act, where aid dollars are used, citizens representative of all socioeconomic and geographical areas of the city are required to be a formal part of the decisionmaking process on where and how these funds are to be spent. These are usually called "citizen action groups" (CAG's). To be used the way it should be, the capital expenditure program, whether or not federally aided, should be carefully planned within the framework of the master plan and public knowledge well in advance of the allocation of any funds. (For further treatment, see "Chapter 8. The Capital Improvements Program.")

IT'S YOU AND ME TOGETHER, BABY

Finally, while we haven't said a great deal about it up to now, the most effective tool of the planning process is citizen involvement—you and me. This participation should begin with the concept of the planning program, be part of its organization and structuring, and continue throughout development, administration, and effectuation of the process. In other words, it is a never-ending challenge to us as citizens yet a must if planning is to be worth the effort. Of particular importance is the role of the individual citizen and neighborhood groups in setting the goals and objectives of the master plan or anything done under the guise of planning. Just what is it planning can and should do for us? What have we now, and what do we want in the way of a community? How can we as citizens play an active role in plan development, administration, and enforcement? These are all questions to which we should have answers before we let ourselves be confident that the planning being done is the way that planning in a democratic society should be done and that we are doing the best we can for our community.

The City of Austin, Texas, has taken this to heart. In the latest attempt to update their master plan, they resolved to make no changes in the plan itself until they had involved the people of the city. Civic leaders were called on to rally as many residents as possible into a task force, and committees and subgroups were formed. After more than two years of discussion, of give-and-take, planning proposals were formulated that, I am told, were given a standing ovation by over 1,000 people assembled at the public presentation.

This brings us back to the essential element—a planning attitude. If we don't see the absolute necessity of improving or want to improve community life and our environment, even if it runs counter-grain to political expediency, we will continue to see ineffective, meaningless usurpation of the plannning process for our cities, counties, regions, and states. The basic principles of planning have to do with improving the general amenities of societal life and making our towns and regions better places in which to live. As each unit grows and develops and fits into the overall pattern of the region, so does the region prosper or wither. Without proper development for municipalities and counties in the states, the areas in which we live and work, and about which we are concerned, cannot grow and prosper. Change of some kind will undoubtedly come to all of the places where we live; some form of development is inevitable. The only question is: What kind of development shall it be?

The choice is, of course, up to the people who live in and govern each. Change can be for better or worse, but there is no such thing as a static community. A community or region will either improve or deteriorate. Hugh Pomeroy, one of my old friends in the planning field, used to delight in taking this point and making a dramatic example in his stirring, evangelistic speeches. He would cite a city that had remained at about 40,000 people for three census enumerations and that therefore felt it was very stable and static. Hugh then went on to show how a careful demographic study had indicated that, while the total population figure may have remained unchanged, internally the city was in a vital, seething state of flux. Age and ethnic changes had taken place, neighborhoods had shifted, the business community had changed in location, and the overall complexion of the city and its people had altered entirely over the years.

Soundly planned areas achieve a desirable degree of stabilization. This stability of development will be seen in any community that has a pattern, that knows where it is going and how it intends to get there. In such a place, planning means a great deal to the individual property owners. They can rest assured that the residences they buy today are protected from an investment standpoint, that their neighborhoods are not going to deteriorate because of undesirable development. At the same time, the overall economic base of the community will be sound because of ample opportunity for the expansion of business and industry.

Having stated what good planning can do and what its legitimate purposes are, I should point out that there are a number of things that planning cannot and should not do. Regrettably, in some cases attempts at the improper use of planning have resulted in failure and misunderstanding of its proper purpose. Planning cannot automatically solve all of the ills of any community. The mere fact that there is a planning commission or even a master plan will not alone result in the correction of past mistakes or even in the prevention of new ones. Planning, to be effective, must be supported by policymaking and an action program. Far too many communities have fallen victim to the illusion that the unveiling of a spanking new plan is the end of all necessary effort and that the mere existence of a plan means that their worries are over.

Planning cannot solve the problems of an outmoded tax structure, nor was it ever intended to. If the taxing system is weak or archaic, nothing in the planning function can fully relieve the undue burden placed upon real estate. Misunderstanding this, many have hopped on the planning bandwagon in the belief that planning can stop development rather than guide it. While it is true that good planning results in more orderly growth, it should never be used to attempt to build a fence around a community and keep others out.

These and many of the other everyday ills of society and our present way of life will not be solved just because we have planning. It is certain, however, that, without some organized effort on the part of all of us to tackle the problems we face from growth and development and to use the collective tools available in a positive way to provide a sense of direction, life will become even more difficult and undesirable. To provide the means for us to see that this does not happen is what community planning is all about.

4. The Planning Commission

It has been interesting over the years to observe the reaction of various individuals upon their initial appointment to a planning commission. Some feel pride and real interest in the opportunity to be of service to the community. These are people who have been and are concerned about the future of urban society. They recognize that major problems exist and that it is going to take concerted citizen involvement to effectuate planned change. They are sincere, dedicated people who, it is hoped, are prepared for the possible frustration of finding that political expediency sometimes has a way of prevailing over logical solutions. On the other hand, many planning commission appointees are very familiar with the politics of government and appointments, far more than they are with the problems of land use, pollution, capital improvement needs, and municipal financing. There have been many who have said, "It's only to be expected that I should be appointed. After all, I've made the right political connections and worked hard for the right party. Besides, I want to run for council, and this is as good a place as any to start." This is prevalent, unfortunately, in far too many of the appointments made and, regretably, something that has held back progress toward improvement from the efforts of the commission.

An even worse impediment to objective and beneficial action is the stacking of the commission with those whose economic livelihoods depend on or can be improved by growth and expansion of the kind achieved at the expense of the community and the general public. I was once involved in a major city with a commission whose membership consisted of two residential real estate brokers, an architect and two engineers who did 90 percent of all new subdivision work in the region, a retired army general, and a junior high school principal. (I never did figure out how the last two made it.) I am sure I don't need to tell you the kind of "planning" action taken by that group. Fortunately, a change in officials, including the election of a woman to the governing body for the first time, improved the composition of the commission.

Those persons who have a desire to do the best possible and who take their responsibility seriously frequently find themselves feeling that they are faced with a quandry. This was best expressed in the comment made by a new planning commission appointee several years ago, which went something like this: "Yesterday I was just an ordinary citizen, and I knew little or nothing about planning. Today I am a member of an official planning commission. I don't feel any different. Was there supposed to be some magic in the swearing-in, and am I now supposed to be an expert? What do I do, and how do I get started?" Fortunately, this person had an inquiring mind and was not satisfied to approach the new task being less than well-informed. Acquiring some-one with that attitude, in all probability the city had picked an excellent planning commission member who rendered valuable service to the community. The fact is, however, that not all new appointees are similarly imbued with the desire for knowledge.

NEXT WEEK WE'VE GOT TO GET ORGANIZED

In order for anyone, planning commission member or just an interested citizen, to understand planning and the duties and responsibilities of a planning commission, it is desirable to understand the theory behind the governmental structure established to facilitate the process. Let's start by remembering that our system of government dictates that the final responsibility for policy, decisionmaking, and action rests with those elected to office to represent us. A cardinal principle in local governmental law in the United States is that, while elected officials may delegate administrative responsibility, legislative authority (decision-making) cannot be delegated. Therefore, there can be no doubt where Harry Truman's old saying "The Buck Stops Here" rests as it applies to the action taken or not taken in our towns. It sits squarely on the elected mayors and council members. As I have said so often, it is not going to assure successful planning just to have a planning commission, regardless of how capable the members of that commission may be. The success will be directly proportionate to the concern, support, understanding of the planning process, and planning attitude of the legislative body.

We have noted that administrative and advisory responsibility can be delegated. We have noted, also, that planning during its early stages was conducted on a rather informal basis. These first efforts came from privately sponsored "committees" or groups of concerned professionals with little or no official status. As urban problems and the nation grew, it became evident that effective results were dependent upon governmental assumption of planning as a legitimate concern. Consequently, the first official planning commissions came into being, beginning in Hartford, Connecticut, in 1907. With this advent of planning as an organized function of government, it became necessary to devise machinery for its operation. The pioneers in the field were strongly of the opinion that mixing planning with politics and the political structure was something to be avoided as much as possible. They were convinced that planning, in order to be meaningful and effective, should be as free as possible of political pressures. The theory was that the agency responsible for the planning process, while being a part of and in direct touch with government, should be to a degree apart from and lifted above routine pressures and political campaigns. The desirability of continuity and of avoiding complete turnovers of entire commissions following elections was stressed; this, too, could be best achieved if the planning function could retain an amount of freedom from the political structure. As planning should be a reflection of the views of the citizens, the early commissions were organized so that the majority, if not all, of the members represented the general public. Thus was born the idea of the lay advisory and recommendatory body, which has carried through to today. In this way, too, the idea was formulated for the local government agency that came to be known as the planning commission or planning board.

As more communities followed the Hartford example, and it became obvious that cities were serious about planning for future growth, state governments began to adopt enabling acts allowing all incorporated units, whether they had home-rule charters or not, to create commissions empowered to make and adopt master plans. By the 1920s, planning, as well as zoning, had grown so rapidly that the U.S. Department of Commerce felt advised to promulgate model state enabling acts for use as guidance in adopting state legislation. The 1928 model for planning accepted the philosophy of the nonpolitical, citizen-dominated commission, to be created by ordinance with members appointed by the mayor. Members of the agency should serve nonconcurrent terms, with a sufficient carryover of a majority of members assured for each succeeding year. The commission should be charged by the governing body in its creating ordinance with the following duties: preparation of planning studies, formulation and adoption of a master plan, provision of advice on zoning and subdivision matters, recommendation of a capital improvements program, and general provision of advice to the elected officials on any other matters referred to it. Many states adopted this model. Even today, when all 50 states have some form of planning legislation for their municipal units, you still will find many provisions of the 1928 prototype setting the rules for this year's planning.

CAN YOU TRUST A POLITICIAN?

No doubt, the pioneers in the planning field felt that they were acting with wisdom to establish the organization responsible for planning the public and private use of land as far outside the political arena as possible. As things have turned out, and with the advantage of hindsight, I must question whether this is the way to have effective planning in today's society. Elected officials are the ones who are going to shape a community and its policies. Whether this is good or bad, it is the political system of the United States, and getting elected to public office (especially getting re-elected) requires a willingness to get involved—or immersed—in politics. As a consequence, the recommendations of a planning commission, frequently not fitting with what may be politically expedient, are often ignored; and planning departments and the commissions themselves lose favor because they are too theoretical, too impractical, and not in tune with the real world. The facts of life are that, regardless of who is on the planning commission and how great the planning proposals may be, the key to implementation rests with the local governing body. They are the ones who adopt the budget (including that for planning activity), pass zoning changes, have final say on what subdivision regulations will be, approve urban renewal projects, and, in general, decide where the city is going and who will do what to get the city there.

This is not to take away from the excellent work that has been done by many planning commissions in the past; nor am I proposing doing away with commissions themselves. Frankly, I don't even have an acceptable alternative to propose. What I am saying, however, is that I am convinced that, whether it is governmental administration or planning, in our system politics is the name of the game. Until we make planning more politically important and politicians more aware that solid support of sound, objective planning is essential to their political careers, we will continue to go through the motions of having planning that in reality pays little more than lip service to the true meaning of the process.

Planning should be an essential part of politics, and politics has to be a part of planning. It is my contention that I was able to do far more for the cause of planning and orderly growth in the minds of the general public as a city manager, and even as an unsuccessful candidate for mayor, than I could have done ever as planning director. If you think that this means that I feel that more people trained in planning should get into politics, you bet your sweet bippy that I do!

YOU'VE GOTTA START SOMEWHERE

If you live in a community that does not have a planning commission, you may wonder how they are started. The actual stimulus for organization at the local level may, and frequently does, come from several directions. Many planning commissions have come into being as a result of the farsightedness and determination of individual mayors or elected council members. In other situations, some form of citizen instigation has resulted in action. A neighborhood organizes because of some crisis that arose, and from this develops the kind of citizen involvement that influences the elected officials to consider an ordinance creating a commission and starting the planning process. Frequently, the spark for action comes from an organized group such as the Junior Chamber of Commerce, the League of Women Voters, or a taxpayers association.

I remember one bedroom community in New Jersey that was being overrun by some of those suburban "dream home" subdivisions, aided and abetted by a governing body rife with private interests. There was no planning or planning commission, and things were going from bad to worse, with schools on double sessions, garbage not being collected and disposed of properly, sidewalks not being required in new developments, and so forth. Two women took it upon themselves to start a crusade against what was happening (or not happening), and the result was a planning commission, a new zoning ordinance, and, at the next election, a new governing body.

Organizations, groups, or even individuals can become effective forces when they become concerned about the way their communities are run and start asking questions. In a very short time, they usually become aware of the fact that planning is the only practical way to cope with the problem of the general future welfare of any area and that the organization of a planning commission is a good way to start. Interested citizens, in turn, arouse others, and the groundswell soon becomes obvious to elected officials, even if they have been less than enthusiastic about the mechanism for long-range comprehensive planning.

In a great many cases, regrettably, communities have not been impressed with the need for action until some particularly unfortunate occurrence in development takes place. This may take the form of a poorly designed and improperly planned subdivision of overwhelming proportions or a piecemeal zoning change to satisfy special interests or a use variance to allow a supermarket in a residential zone or even the pollution of water supplies. I well remember a community whose officials I had attempted on many occasions to interest in planning in advance of the building boom. They would have none of it—could not, in fact, be bothered even to prepare and enact a zoning ordinance. Shortly after World War II, the community underwent development at an astronomical rate. Three thousand homes were built in two years, many of them on 6,000-square-foot lots with individual septic tanks. Unfortunately, the underlying soil was practically impervious hardpan, and the resulting health hazards soon became obvious. When seepage began to trickle through the subdivision streets and the pavement itself began to slide downhill, the community woke up. Needless to say, there was a great scurry to organize a planning board and to enact a zoning ordinance. Through haste, the community obtained a zoning ordinance of lower quality than it should have, and much of the time and energy spent on planning was wasted. No zoning could have corrected the multiplicity of errors that had been allowed to occur.

Fortunately, this situation is less likely to happen now, largely due to the action of the federal government. We have mentioned the entrance of Washington influence on local planning through the financial assistance provided for plan development through Section 701 of the Federal Housing Act of 1954. This legislation also placed the government squarely in the position of midwifing the births of new planning commissions. Municipalities were told that in order to qualify for the aid dollars they would have to be able to show that they had ongoing planning or were in the process of obtaining it. Nothing speaks more strongly or offers more inducement for local action than the strings tied to federal monetary assistance. No local elected official wants to be in the position of facing the accusation from some of the "outs" that the "ins," by inaction, are causing a loss of the opportunity of Washington's largesse. This has become an even stronger incentive for the mechanism for local planning over the years since 1954. Every federally funded program since, including the "Model Cities" program, revenue sharing, and the Community Development Act, has carried with it this message: "Do some long-range planning and get citizens involved if you want federal aid."

As a result, few urban places today are without some form of planning and a planning commission. Whether this somewhat coerced action has been effective and objective and whether sensible planning has been pursued with enthusiasm in every case are different questions. In fact, these are the questions all of us should be asking ourselves now if we live where there is a planning commission. Have the commission and the elected officials really had their heart in the process, or has it been something done just to play the federal grantsmanship game? Have results occurred that have improved the environment, the quality of life, and the community character? Do the citizens know what planning is being done and who is doing it, and do they understand and support it? These and many other questions need to be asked and answered positively before anyone is satisfied with just an "Oh yes, we have planning." The federal agencies have provided us with the mechanism through their requirements, but it is up to us to be sure that we truly have an effective process.

SETTING THE STAGE FOR PLANNING ACTION

Regardless of motivation or stimulation, the first necessary step under the state enabling acts is for the governing body to pass an ordinance creating a planning commission, establishing its membership, and out-

lining its responsibilities. Once a planning commission has been organized, there is still the question of where it fits into the organizational
structure of the community. Normally, enabling acts indicate that most
of the members are to be appointed by the mayor; the appointments
may or may not be subject to the approval of the governing body,
depending upon the particular enabling act. In the case of the mayor-
council form of government, it is usually understood that the planning
commission is a part of the administrative office of the mayor. Although
reporting to the council generally, it is primarily responsible to the
mayor. This, at least, is the position that the planning function should
occupy. In the council-manager structure, the appointments are usually
made by the council, and, while the manager works closely with the
commission, it is primarily responsible to the council. The arrangement
in other types of governmental structure may vary slightly, but primarily the planning commission is considered to be a citizen advisory arm to
the policymakers and to the chief executive officer.

To aid the planning commission in its work, most communities
also create a complete department of planning with a staff, just as there
is a department of public works or recreation. This department may
consist of only a professional planner and some administrative assis-
tants, or it may include a large number of trained and supportive
personnel. Presently, such departments have a dual responsibility. They
must work closely with the appointed planning commission, providing
them with information upon which to make recommendations. They
also must work cooperatively with the elected officials, the mayor,
and/or city manager. This dual responsibility can place the planning
director in the awkward position of having to resolve conflicting views
relating to theoretical planning and pragmatic politics. It is a capable
planning director who can avoid being damagingly caught in this cross-
fire. Having been the planning director, upon becoming the city manager in Albuquerque I have to admit to having had an even closer relation
with the planning department than did either the planning commission
or the council. We even went so far as to organize all department heads
into a task force to work with the planning director through once-a-
week meetings, just to talk about planning for the future city and its
needs. It was unthinkable, but it worked!

As a result of moves such as this to incorporate planning more into
management, it has been suggested by some that a separate agency for
planning in the form of a commission is no longer necessary and that the

function and the department should be part of the chief executive's office. The arguments for this include the proposal that effective planning is really a part of management, that coordination is better achieved in this manner, and that all planning proposals should be closely related to the municipal budget. As a consequence, many feel that a better approach would be to have all planning responsibility placed with the chief executive, with a PPBS (Planning, Programming, and Budget System) being the means for putting it all together. The mayor or manager would then work with council, utilizing a broader citizen's advisory group or groups to be sure of having citizen input and opinion. Here again the federal government has played a strong role in encouraging planning by management rather than by agencies not directly responsible to the electorate. In recent programs, all federal departments have been insistent that the chief executive not only be involved but also be the one held responsible for the effectiveness of any federally funded program. This discussion as to which is the best approach will continue for some time, with both methods being used. By no means, however, is the day of the independent planning commission over. It is still a very good, effective approach for smaller communities and rural areas.

Regardless of whether planning is advisory or a part of management, the important thing is to be sure that the process established is meaningful and has the full support of the elected officials. This needs to be more than just tacit endorsement and certainly more than mere acquiescence under pressure to create a planning program. Although it is infrequent, I have known of situations where elected officials basically opposed to the idea of organized planning went through the motion of establishing the process with the full intent of seeing that it failed so that they could put an end to "this planning nonsense" once and for all. Such an occurrence took place several years ago in an eastern Pennsylvania county where a county planning program was inaugurated and a planning director hired at the insistence of interested citizens. The planning director spent a year fighting a losing battle against complete isolation and a ridiculously low budget. He was assigned a room in the county courthouse but was unable to obtain furniture and was not even permitted to have a telephone. After a few months of going to the corner phone booth to make calls, he moved on to greener pastures and the county planning program folded.

Happily, this story is the exception rather than the rule. Where planning is supported intelligently, the duties and responsibilities of the planning commission are the subject of public discussion. Of course, as its name implies, the first responsibility of the agency is to plan. It must develop thoughtful plans for the future provision of municipal services and for the development of the total community. Planning is an organized process geared to provide the best possible blueprint for the most efficient municipal action. It is not just collective thinking or spur-of-the-moment decisionmaking. One of the delusions to which certain planning commission board members are subject is that no special preparation is necessary to understand planning: their position alone confers clairvoyance upon them. Regardless of the sincerity of individual members, and regardless of their basic familiarity with the community, "planning" that is merely collective thinking without investigation and analysis is both insufficient and ineffective.

PUTTING THE AVAILABLE TOOLS TO WORK

The work of a planning commission usually takes the form of the organization of a master plan or a development plan. The term "master plan" was devised to indicate comprehensiveness during the early days of planning and has been the one in most common use. It is the term that has been incorporated in most of the state enabling acts, and it has received considerable acceptance as an appropriate designation of the culmination of the planning process by the courts of this country.

In addition to the development of the master plan, planning includes the more commonly understood and accepted legal document known as the zoning ordinance. Zoning is an effectuating tool of a plan or project for future community growth. It is extremely important that zoning be kept in tune with the plan and that it reflect the latest consideration available through the planning process. The control and regulation of subdivision activity within the community is also a function of the planning process. The planning commission is usually the administrative agency authorized to review and possibly even approve the subdivision of land. This, too, must be closely coordinated with overall planning activity. As part of the master plan, proposals will be made for the provision of future public facilities. The projection of the cost of facilities and when they should be provided is part of the capital improvements program, which is, in turn, a part of planning. (The basic tools of planning are discussed in greater detail in the following chapters.)

Because planning deals with future streets and roads as well as existing ones, some planning statutes provide that the development of an official map of the municipality shall be included within the prerogatives of the planning commission. The actual adoption of such an official map, which is binding as to street locations and rights-of-way, is usually a function of the governing body, and official maps are ordinarily adopted by the enactment of an ordinance. Many state enabling acts also provide for the referral of other matters to a planning commission at the discretion of elected officials or public agencies. A variety of duties have thus been assigned, including such things as suggesting revisions for building codes, surveying overlapping street names and suggesting a renaming program, studying the efficiency of the garbage disposal method practiced by the municipality, and determining whether a sanitary land-fill operation can be made to go within the community.

Whatever the program undertaken by a planning commission, it should have as its primary motive the careful formulation of a master plan. The commission should always remember that the program is basically one of coordinating and pulling together various ideas concerned with the development of the community. The desired comprehensiveness can be obtained only if the planning commission has at its disposal adequate information to reach an intelligent decision. Once a commission is organized and begins to familiarize itself with its role, there is usually a concern about its administration. Frequently members have been frustrated and confused because they have been left to fend for themselves within the municipal administration. They have hesitated to assume initiative and have not been at all sure just what was expected of them. Any planning commission member should understand that, once organized, the responsibility for initiating a program and general administration should be accepted by the commission. This does not mean that activity contrary to the policies of the established local government should be undertaken.

The commission, however, should make certain that it does not permit itself to become simply a rubber-stamp organization, simply adding legitimacy to any action taken or requested by the governing body or administrative departments. The role of the commission should be that of studying, proposing, and even criticizing where necessary. It must be remembered that the real function is to make certain that the best interests of the entire community are being protected and enhanced. That is a far cry from the situation that I ran into in one eastern city when I was called in to discuss the possibility of a consulting job. Upon arrival at the appointed place, I discovered only the mayor, the president of council, and the city attorney present. When I asked about the planning commission and their role in the project, I was informed that they met only on call and that I really should not worry about them. I am happy to report that I was gracious enough to allow another consultant to have the pleasure of that contract.

Normally, a properly organized planning commission meets on a regularly scheduled basis at least once a month. Many meet more frequently, and some of the best ones that I have known have one regular monthly pubic meeting and one or two monthly work sessions. These work sessions are primarily for the commission itself and are used to do the actual planning work. During that time, they meet with their staff and/or consultants or hear reports of subcommittees and then consider action that can and should be taken. In this way, they are able to handle routine assignments and still not lose sight of long-range objectives. An efficient commission normally has its own set of by-laws. The by-laws establish the time and place of meetings, the officers, the subcommittees, and the procedure for conducting business. A helpful model set of by-laws can usually be obtained from the state agency concerned with planning, a state league of municipalities, or such national organizations as the American Planning Association. As is the case with model forms of any kind, these by-laws should not be copied verbatim but may be used as the basis for the formulation of a specific set of procedures with the advice of the municipal attorney.

The important thing is for each planning commission to know where it is going and just how it is going to get there. A definite procedure and a formal organization will go a long way toward making a smooth operation. Subdividers should know exactly what is expected of them and how they can get their subdivision plats processed. Any citizen or citizen group should know that they can be heard and when and how this can take place. Anyone interested in having a public hearing conducted should be able to find out quickly how it can be done and how it will be run when it is scheduled. While the commission should be careful not to overload itself with administrative detail, it should be equally careful that it does not permit itself to operate in a slipshod fashion.

GETTING ALONG WITH OTHERS TAKES PLANNING TOO

Another vital question of concern in the operation is that of the relationship to the governing body and other officials of the community. Because the primary role of the planning commission is an advisory one to the governing body, the relationship between these two groups must, of necessity, be cooperative and extremely close. Mayors and councils or city commissioners should keep the commission informed of their problems and their progress. Conversely, the planning commission that does not have a close liaison with elected officials is doomed to failure. Some years ago, I had experience with just such an example of this lack of liaison in a Delaware community. Operating under a city charter, the planning commission was totally separate from the governing body. The planning agency had spent some four years in building a working vocabulary of planning and in thoroughly understanding the problems of the community. They now were extremely enthusiastic about the development of a comprehensive master plan and an urban renewal program. Unfortunately, because no one from the governing body had been in on the discussions, this same enthusiasm had not been gained by the elected officials. The result was that there was resentment on the part of these officials against the planning commission's zeal and a feeling that a master plan was just a means of wasting money.

On the other hand, the inclusion of elected officials as members of the planning commission does not always guarantee the necessary support. I once worked with a community where members of the governing body were on the planning commission and met with us regularly to discuss the formulation of a master plan. As commission members, they either kept silent or tacitly supported the proposals. When they put on the caps of elected officials, they each assumed an entirely different character and opposed the action taken, giving the impression that it was all entirely new to them.

The proper relationship between the governing body and the planning commission is that of a corporation's board of directors with its technical advisory committee. If the proper aims of both groups are diligently pursued, the results can be extremely successful. The governing body cannot, of course, give up its policymaking role, nor can it delegate legislative authority. It can, however, make valuable use of its technical advisory arm, the planning commission.

The employees of the municipal government also should be made to feel a part of the planning program. The work of the municipal engineer, the building inspector, and the zoning officer are integral parts of planning activity. In many cases, these positions are filled by devoted public servants who have, over a long period of time, gained a tremendous insight into the problems of the community. Their special skills are invaluable in effectuating the decisions reached in the planning program. Again, the proper relationship is one of cooperation and close liaison.

What you do when this is impossible due to the individuals involved is another matter, especially if you don't have the support of the governing body. Many times long-tenured bureaucratic department heads have built up an even greater political power base than some of the elected officials and operate in their own little independent empires. I have known of a city manager who was very planning conscious and attempted to get this kind of cooperation for planning from all department heads. The director of public works who had been there much longer than that city manager was not about to do anything he thought would weaken his baronistic fief. He told the manager so and further added that he had seen city managers come and go and he would be around long after his present antagonist was gone. Sure enough, he was right; he is still there but the manager is long gone. The moral: Don't think you can buck entrenched bureaucrats if you don't have the muscle.

The commission must also be prepared to deal with other public agencies. The good member will understand that the development of a master plan or the formulation of a coordinated planning program cuts across the areas of responsibility of the school board, the urban renewal authority, the parking authority, the board of health, the zoning board of appeals, and many other agencies. All of these agencies are concerned with specialized functions of government. They feel, and justifiably, that their functions are important: they cannot be ignored if the planning program is to be successful. The commission must learn to assume a coordinating role tactfully and without creating a feeling of interference.

The planning commission must also recognize its responsibility to keep the public informed. The activities of the commission should be a matter of public knowledge if citizens are to reach intelligent conclusions on planning matters. The best cure for rumor mongering and emotional reactions is preventive: get the facts on the public record first.

Depending upon the requirements of the state enabling act, the planning commission is ordinarily made up of five to nine persons, and membership is divided between appointed citizens and elected officials of the municipality. In most cases, the majority of the commission is comprised of appointed members holding no elected office within the municipality. The success or failure of the planning function is to great degree dependent upon the qualifications and characteristics of each member. I have been asked many times to define the best type of person for membership on a planning commission. This is an extremely difficult assignment and one that I have constantly sought to duck. There is, of course, no one best candidate for membership. Although the individual's knowledge and experience are important considerations, they are secondary to a genuine interest in the community's problems. Persons trained in architecture, engineering, law, economics, sociology, and business administration make good members. But so do other citizens, including the woman who works at home. The test of probable success is devotion and honest concern, far more than a specialized background. It is much easier to identify the one trait that should preclude appointment. This, of course, is a selfish interest, expressed through political ambition and a desire for personal gain or self-aggrandizement.

A planning commission and its resultant program will be no better than the raw material used in its construction. In this case, the raw material is the quality of the personnel selected.

5. The Master Plan

The next chapters will discuss the four traditional basic tools of the planning process. These are the master plan, zoning, subdivision controls, and capital improvements programming. While there are those who say that these avenues available to local governments to aid in development and land management are no longer as effective as is needed, they are still the major processes recognized by state enabling acts. They are the legal foundation upon which all other approaches and techniques must be based, whether we are talking about growth management, performance zoning, planned unit developments, transfer of development rights, or any of the other modern, flexible approaches to land-use regulation. All elements of planning, even most of the social concerns, are anchored upon or affected by the way in which land is used. Community character is set, general economic well-being is built, cultural and social amenities are provided, and ease and convenience of circulation are determined—all by what occurs on the building blocks of land parcels fitted together like a jigsaw puzzle to make the total environment of any urban area. Fundamental to the ability of the general populace or the community to do anything about this urban environment, to shape it in accordance with principles and thought out objective still is some idea of a blueprint for growth—the master plan. It may be called a development plan, a comprehensive plan, a general plan, or any of several other terms that have come into popular usage in recent years; but if it is to be official and legal by state statutes and acceptable by the courts as a basis to defend against a legal challenge of enacted land controls, it is still the master plan.

UNDERSTANDING IS NOT ALWAYS EASY

Even though the term and the process have been around for many years, there are many people who have no idea of what it is, what its purpose and objectives are, what it looks like, or, if meaningful, what far-reaching effects it has on individual and community lives. There are probably very few cities of any size that do not have, or have not had prepared, something called a master plan. Yet a random survey of any 100 people on any main street, asking them whether their community has such a plan and whether they are familiar with it, would produce some extremely disappointing results. This comes back to one of the primary problems of planning in this country. We have had to face the necessity of developing something that can be used by government to direct the private use of land before we have done the job we should have done in educating people about this necessity and the process. When we find those who know about planning, we still find that they lack knowledge about a master plan and what it can and should do. Many times when I hear a person attempt to offer an impression of a master plan, I am reminded of the story of the blind men and the elephant: it seems that the understanding of the term depends upon the particular part of the animal being touched and with which there is a degree of familiarity.

To help in knowing what to look for, and so that we will all have a better chance to get in touch with the same piece of the "elephant," I have frequently suggested a number of things one should expect to find. First of all there should be printed material giving a reasonably concise summary of the plan and the process of its formulation. Included should be goals and objectives of the overall plan and each of its parts. These parts should cover such things as population and demography, land use, traffic and circulation, parks and open space, housing, utilities and services, drainage, social programs, urban design standards, and general cultural characteristics—both present and future. In the definition of future needs, specific ways should be indicated for carrying out the proposals and seeing that they become reality. There should be a clear discussion of what, why, where, and when with regard to everything advocated for the future community. There should also be evidence of the amount of involvement of the public, the local administration, and the elected officials in the preparation as well as in the effectuation to date. (I may add that if the master plan doesn't do this, perhaps we need to think about getting involved and helping to see that it does. See the discussion below of Florida's Local Government Comprehensive Planning Act of 1975 for everything you always wanted to know about a master plan but were afraid to ask.)

To better understand what the master plan is, or should be, perhaps we should start with an exploration of the desirable objectives and purpose. Simply stated, they are the same as that of the planning process—to shape a better community and to avoid costly and undesirable mistakes detrimental to the well-being of the public interest. The master plan is the tangible expression of how this is to be done. It should depict verbally and graphically all that anyone would need to know to understand what studies have been made, what problems need to be solved, and steps that need to be taken to accomplish the objectives. As to the latter, the foundation of the plan's proposals and objectives should be goals that have been established through citizen involvement. In other words, a good master plan should be the means whereby the people, working with the planning commission and professional staff, have said, "This is what we know our community is today—the good and the bad—and this is what we want to see it become in five or 10 years."

DEFINITIONS REVISITED

There has been much written about master plans with many definitions given. What I have said to this point is only an attempt at a general concept summary. Actually, just what the master plan is and should or can do depends to a large extent upon the state legislature and the wording used in the enabling act it passes. Even though there is a great deal of similarity from state to state, specific items covered do vary according to each state's interests and tradition. It is recommended that anyone interested in knowing more about the legal status of a plan and what an adopted plan should contain obtain a copy of the state planning enabling act and carefully read its provisions. These state acts are very good sources of information, and, in most cases, a lot of good thought has gone into their preparation. As an indication of this, reference will be made to three of these acts for further explanation of the purpose and objectives of a master plan and the kinds of things that should be included but, even more importantly, to show how the philosophy behind planning and the process has changed in the last 10 to 15 years.

The first example is an older act passed in New Jersey in 1953, since revised and updated. Those involved with its formulation wanted to have the most modern and best definition and statement of purpose possible. For the state of the art at that time, they did achieve this. The definition read:

> ... a master plan for the physical development of the municipality shall comprise land use, circulation and a report presenting the objectives, assumptions, standards and principles which are embodied in the various interlocking portions of the master plan. The master plan shall be a composite of the one or more mapped and written proposals recommending the physical development of the municipality which the planning board shall have adopted either as a whole or severally after public hearing. Such master plan may include proposals for various stages in the future development of the municipality.

To provide additional clarification of the scope and purpose, after listing a number of individual areas of concern that could be included in the plan studies, the legislation then stated:

> In the preparation of the master plan, the planning board shall give due consideration to the probable ability of the municipality to carry out, over a period of years, the various public or quasi-public projects embraced in the plan without the imposition of unreasonable financial burdens. In such preparation, the planning board shall cause to be made careful and comprehensive surveys and studies of present conditions and the prospects for future growth of the municipality. The master plan shall be made with the general purpose of guiding and accomplishing a coordinated, adjusted, and harmonious development of the municipality....

This certainly gave a good idea of just what a master plan was all about and for many years provided a sense of direction for New Jersey municipalities. A careful reading, however, and some thorough application to the scope of community concerns today and the things with which truly effective master planning must deal, clearly indicates that the scope must be much broader. It is to be noted that in 1953 the emphasis was still almost exclusively on the physical aspects of development. Very little was specifically said about social concerns and problems, environmental considerations, or citizen and community involvement. Compare this to the following excerpts taken from Florida's Local Government Comprehensive Planning Act of 1975 (Chapter 75-257, Laws of Florida). Under "Section 2, Intent and Purpose," there are six separate statements, the first two of which read:

(1) In conformity with and in furtherance of the purpose of the Florida Environmental Land and Water Management Act of 1972, chapter 380, Florida Statutes, it is the purpose of this act to utilize and strengthen the existing role, processes, and powers of local governments in Florida in the establishment and implementation of comprehensive planning programs to guide and control future development.

(2) It is the intent of this act that its adoption is necessary so that Florida local governments can preserve and enhance present advantages; encourage the most appropriate use of land, water, and resources consistent with the public interest; overcome present handicaps; and deal effectively with future problems that may result from the use and development of land within their jurisdictions. Through the process of comprehensive planning, it is intended that Florida units of local government can preserve, promote, protect, and improve the public health, safety, comfort, good order, appearance, convenience, law enforcement and fire prevention, and general welfare; prevent the overcrowding of land and avoid undue concentration of population; facilitate the adequate and efficient provision of transportation, water, sewerage, schools, parks, recreational facilities, housing and other requirements and services; and conserve, develop, utilize, and protect natural resources within their jurisdictions.

Having set forth the purpose rather carefully, the act proceeds to state that before July 1, 1976, each unit of local government must have designated a planning agency, which, before July 1, 1979, must have prepared and adopted "a comprehensive plan of the type and in the manner set out in the act." Earlier, local government had been defined as meaning "any county or municipality or any special district or local governmental entity established pursuant to law which exercises regulatory authority over and grants development permits for land development." Again, we see a far-reaching charge.

THE INGREDIENTS DETERMINE THE QUALITY OF THE PRODUCT

Next, the act says that in the preparation of these comprehensive (master) plans, there are 14 areas of concern, or "elements," that must be included in the planning for all local government units and 12 others that are "optional" but advised for communities under 50,000 in population and required for all others. The mandatory coverage for all units includes the following:

(1) The comprehensive plan shall consist of materials in such descriptive form, written or graphic, as may be appropriate to the prescription of principles, guidelines, and standards for the orderly and balanced future economic, social, physical, environmental, and fiscal development of the area.

(2) Coordination of the several elements of the local comprehensive plan shall be a major objective of the planning process. . . .

(3) The economic assumptions on which the plan is based and any amendments thereto shall be analyzed and set out as a part of the plan. . . .

(4) Coordination of the local comprehensive plan with the comprehensive plans of adjacent municipalities, of the county or adjacent counties or region, and to the state comprehensive plan shall be a major objective of the local comprehensive planning process. . . .

(5) The comprehensive plan and its elements shall contain policy recommendations for the implementation of the plan and its elements.

(6) In addition to the general requirements of subsections (1)

through (5) of this section, the comprehensive plan shall include the following elements:

(a) A future land use plan element designating proposed future general distribution, location, and extent of the uses of land for housing, business, industry, agriculture, recreation, conservation, education, public buildings and grounds, other public facilities, and other categories of the public and private uses of land. . . .

(b) A traffic circulation element consisting of the types, locations, and extent of existing and proposed major thoroughfares and transportation routes.

(c) A general sanitary sewer, solid waste, drainage, and potable water element correlated to principles and guidelines for future land use. . . .

(d) A conservation element for the conservation, development, utilization, and protection of natural resources in the area. . . .

(e) A recreation and open space element indicating a comprehensive system of public and private sites for recreation. . . .

(f) A housing element consisting of standards, plans and principles to be followed in the provision of housing for existing residents and the anticipated population growth of the area. . . .

(g) For those units of local government lying in part or in whole in the coastal zone as defined by the Coastal Zone Management Act of 1972, volume 16, United States Code s. 1453(a), a coastal zone protection element. . . .

(h) An intergovernmental coordination element showing relationships and stating principles and guidelines to be used in the accomplishment of coordination of the adopted comprehensive plan with the plans of school boards and other units of local government providing services but not having regulatory authority over the use of land. . . .

(i) A utility element in conformance with the ten year site plan of the Florida Electrical Power Plant Siting Act, Part II, chapter 403.

Those additional items that must be included in the larger communities' planning and that may be part of any plan are:

(a) ... a mass transit element showing proposed methods for the moving of people, rights of way, terminals, related facilities, and fiscal considerations for the accomplishment of the element.

(b) ... plans for port, aviation and related facilities coordinated with the general circulation and transportation element.

(c) ... a plan element for the circulation of non-automotive vehicular and pedestrian traffic including bicycle paths and bikeways, exercise trails, riding facilities, and such other matters as may be related to the improvement and safety of movement of all types of vehicular and pedestrian traffic or to recreational aspects of circulation.

(d) ... a plan element for the development of off-street parking facilities for motor vehicles and the fiscal considerations for the accomplishment of the element.

(e) A public services and facilities element (not including solid waste, drainage, and sewer which is a required element under paragraph (c) of subsection (6) or plans required by paragraph (i) of subsection (6) of this section) showing general plans for local utilities, and rights of way easements, and facilities.

(f) A public buildings and related facilities element showing locations and arrangements of civic and community centers, public schools, hospitals, libraries, police and fire stations and other public buildings. ...

(g) A recommended community design element which may consist of design recommendations for land subdivision, neighborhood development and redevelopment, design of open space locations, and similar matters. ...

(h) A general area redevelopment element consisting of plans and programs for the redevelopment of slums and blighted locations in the area. . . .

(i) A safety element for the protection of residents and property of the area from fire, hurricane, or man-made or natural catastrophe.

(j) An historical and scenic preservation element setting out plans and programs for those structures or lands in the area having historical, archaeological, architectural, scenic, or similar significance.

(k) An economic element setting forth principles and guidelines for the commercial and industrial development, if any, and the employment and manpower utilization within the area.

(l) Such other elements as may be peculiar to and necessary for the area concerned and as are added to the comprehensive plan by the governing body upon the recommendation of the local planning agency.

This comprehensive list of concerns is a far cry from the simplicity of the model enabling act suggested by the U.S. Department of Commerce in 1928. Yet investigation will disclose that many of our states, particularly those in the Southwest and Midwest, are still satisfied to allow their cities to attempt to deal with the complexity of today's planning problems with legislation patterned after the model and enacted by them in the 1930s or 1940s. How commendable it is to see a state like Florida recognize that conservation, housing, ecology, and community design can and should be a part of a master plan. And, lest I get into trouble with some of my good New Jersey friends, let it be noted also that my use of the New Jersey act of 1953 was in no way intended to imply that this is the way that state has left its legislation or that it is among those operating with outmoded tools. New Jersey has long been one of the leaders in planning and land-control legislation; it has, since 1953, taken many progressive steps in this area, including the creation of a state department of community affairs and the passage of some very far-reaching statewide land-use-control measures. Looking at the 1953 New Jersey act in relation to Florida's more recent plan, one can see the comparative evolution of our thinking from the period

1928-53 to 1975. I am extremely impressed with the Florida legislation and would commend it for careful consideration as a guide for updating and revising planning in other states.

NOW THAT WE KNOW WHAT, HOW DO WE DO IT?

Once it has been generally accepted as to what a master plan comprises, the next question usually asked by most planning commission members is, "How do we get one?" There is nothing to prevent a community from preparing a master plan with the talent of the local commission. This has been done in some cases, usually where there are a number of extremely devoted and civic-minded members. The do-it-yourself master plan is, however, extremely difficult to achieve. The probability that any member will have sufficient time to gather the essential information and material is very small. At the same time, the preparation of a competent plan requires a high degree of technical knowledge that is not usually found among citizen appointees. While it is true that members can broaden the scope of their technical information, the time available for study is limited. The best method of obtaining a master plan thus resolves itself into a matter of securing competent professional help. The technical personnel can be made available either on a permanent staff basis or from a planning consulting firm. The permanent staff is usually employed by the city and is responsible to the planning commission. If a consulting service is to be used, the consultant is also engaged by the city and works directly with the commission. (For a more complete discussion, see "Chapter 9. The Care and Feeding of Planning Professionals.")

Still another way for a local government unit to secure professional help and technical assistance is frequently found through state, regional, or county planning agencies. Almost all states have an organization charged with state planning activity and may have arranged for their staff to actually perform some of the services needed to develop local plans. Even more involved in assisting local planning action are the regional and county organizations. In some areas, communities can contract to have the professional staffs of such groups undertake studies or prepare a complete master plan. In the past several years, through the Federal Office of Management and Budget's A-95 review process, regional councils of government and regional planning commissions have been encouraged as a means of coordination and review of federally funded projects. While this has stimulated their formulation and federal aid for planning and other programs has assisted in providing their budgets, these agencies have had a fundamental purpose of promoting and aiding local planning activity. Some people have resisted and resented the efforts of these agencies, feeling that this is just another attempt of "big government" to take over and run local affairs. Though there may be some justification for this feeling, it must be remembered that successful planning at the local level requires cooperation between all affected governments and coordination of activity and development policies between local, county, regional, and state agencies.

Even with all of this discussion about the purpose of a master plan, what it is, and how it is put together, perhaps we still need to say something about the form and format. What does it look like? Actually, they can take a wide variety of forms. Usually, regardless of the approach taken, there will be a printed summary for public distribution. This will, or should, include written text, statistical tables, charts, graphs, and graphic depiction of the community and the proposals. There is always a master plan report or reports explaining the studies undertaken, the findings, conclusions, and recommendations. Also, there should be a clear discussion of how citizens were involved in the plan formulation. Did suggestions come from neighborhoods, were citizen organizations contacted and did they participate, and was there a concerted and structured effort made to develop the goals and objectives of the plan from this effort? Regardless of how derived, these should have been or should be the basis of any plan proposals. The final product can be put together in any number of physical forms, shapes, and sizes. There are big ones, fat ones, color-printed ones, little ones, and summary ones. Due to the cost involved in printing and distribution, it may be difficult for all of the background material to be included in whatever product is made available generally. Those who are genuinely interested should know where all of the documents can be studied, and easy access to them should be provided.

During my consulting days, in order to try to get information about plans and their proposals into the hands of as many people as possible, I encouraged communities to print plan summaries in newspaper tabloid form. These could be folded into convenient mailing pieces, run through the tax assessor's office for addressing, and sent to everyone on the tax rolls. Of course, other copies were kept available for people to pick up and were distributed to apartment renters. On a few occasions, local newspapers were cooperative enough to print such tabloids and distribute them free of charge. In several places, a brief citizen questionnaire was utilized to solicit reaction and further input.

TRADITIONAL VERSUS POLICIES MASTER PLANS

At this point, some comments seem in order regarding the debate that has been going on for some time concerning the relative merit of the form and format of a master plan. This centers around the question of whether or not the traditional master plan, with its physical depiction of present conditions, resources, and proposed changes directed toward long-range propositions, is really valid in meeting today's needs. Those who say otherwise support the idea of a "policies" plan that concentrates on examining present conditions and problems, establishes policies to deal with these, and then recommends specific techniques and priorities for changes and improvement. The policies plan may be presented in text form but will have supporting graphics, charts, and tables, which may or may not be included in that which is made available to the public at large. Many will present the master plan in separate sections, with one devoted to policy questions, one to the physical capital needs and improvements, one to social programs, and one to suggested and recommended effectuation ordinance adoption or amendments. (Samples of the policies sections from the master plans of Denver, Colorado, and Albuquerque, New Mexico, are given in "Appendix A" to give an idea of what a policies plan looks like.)

Supporters of this approach believe that people are much more interested in today and that it is more important to deal with the pragmatic immediate problems of community life than to have fancy colored pictures of idealistic schemes for future land use and facilities projected for anywhere from five to 25 years in the future. On the other hand, those who defend the traditional master plan are equally convinced that planning that is not long-range and does not project a vision for the future gives little sense of direction and falls short of providing needed inspiration. For what it's worth, my own belief is that the best answer lies somewhere between the two extremes. Planning, to be comprehensive, should be long-range, but there also should be a divisional time frame relating to immediate goal achievement by policy changes. The best plans in the future will be those that separate long-range capital expenditures for physical facilities and improvements necessary for social, cultural, environmental, and economic betterment from a well-stated set of immediate and midrange policy statements with priority establishment.

WHAT TO DO UNTIL THE BABY ARRIVES

Another question that arises frequently is in regard to the time required to obtain a master plan. It usually takes from 12 to 24 months to complete a thorough master planning project. In the meantime, the problems of the community go on. What concerns the commission members is what to do until the master plan comes. It seems to me that the first and probably best bit of advice is be cautious, but do not panic. Development and growth cannot be stopped. Decisions will have to be made that in many cases will have an effect on the master plan. Care should therefore be exercised to make certain that sufficient consideration is given to each proposal and that each member is conscious of the meaning of the pending master plan. While the plan is being prepared, there are many other things that can be done. Independent investigation of planning principles in general and the reading of publications regarding master plans and planning would be extremely valuable. On numerous occasions, I have discovered that planning board members in various communities have never even read the state enabling act authorizing their activity. The attitude seems to be that because it is a law, it is in the domain of the lawyers alone. This, of course, is not so; reading the enabling act will provide a great deal of information and a better understanding of the duties and responsibilities of the commission.

The planning commission member who is conscientious should become even more familiar with the community and its characteristics. While he or she may have lived there a number of years, the individual probably will be surprised by the many tangible and intangible characteristics that have gone unobserved until looked at through planning eyes. Trips into various parts of the municipality both alone and with other members will be extremely helpful. At the same time, it should be stressed that it is of vital importance for the commission member to be completely familiar with the work that is going on regarding the master plan. Discussions, meetings, visits to the planning office, and reading of memoranda and reports are important.

I have seen commission members fail to read a single report submitted to them during the development of a master plan. I remember, for example, one man who sat through six meetings discussing a future land-use plan without saying a word and who afterward, at the time of a public hearing at which a few objectors had expressed opposition, jumped up and proclaimed that he had been against the proposal all along. It is also a common occurrence to be asked a specific question and to point out to the member doing the questioning that a detailed explanation is provided on page 15 of the report submitted two weeks ago. Yes, there is a great deal that can be done until the master plan comes. There is, of course, a great deal more than can be done after it comes.

NOW, LET'S MAKE IT LEGAL

Once a plan has been prepared, it should be adopted and given some official status. The procedure for doing this varies from state to state, and, again, the enabling act should be consulted. To the surprise of many, in most states the plan does not have to be adopted by the governing body; this action is the function of the planning commission. Following the idea that master plans should be advisory and therefore not legislated as such, most of the legislative acts say that the planning commission may adopt all or a part of the master plan by resolution and that amendments to the plan may be made the same way. Before this can be done, there must be a public hearing. As an illustration of the adoption procedure, note the following section from Colorado's enabling act:

> 31-23-208. *Procedure of Commission.* The commission may adopt the plan as a whole by a single resolution or may by successive resolutions adopt successive parts of the plan (said parts corresponding with major geographical sections or divisions of the municipality or with functional subdivisions of the subject matter of the plan), and may adopt any amendment or extension thereof or addition thereto. Before the adoption of the

plan or any such part, amendment, extension, or addition, the commission shall hold at least one public hearing thereon, notice of the time and place of which shall be given by one publication in a newspaper of general circulation in the municipality and in the official newspaper of the county affected. The adoption of the plan, any part, amendment, extension, or addition shall be by resolution of the commission carried by the affirmative votes of not less than two-thirds of the entire membership of the commission. The resolution shall refer expressly to the maps and descriptive and other matter intended by the commission to form the whole or part of the plan, and the action taken shall be recorded on the map and plan and descriptive matter by the identifying signature of the chairman or secretary of the commission. An attested copy of the plan or part thereof shall be certified to each governmental body of the territory affected and after the approval by each body shall be filed with the county clerk and recorder of each county wherein the territory is located.

In spite of the above and the fact that most states do not require any other action, many places feel that the plan should be acted upon by the governing body. Thus, in some cases councils pass and mayors sign resolutions adopting the plan. This may be good supportive action, even when not required by statute, but I am much more interested in seeing elected officials support the plan by taking effective action, employing such tools as zoning, and insisting that the plan be followed by department heads. The plan—and I—can do without ceremonial fluff designed to imply "official" legitimacy and sanction.

With the adoption of the plan comes the question of legal status. Does a master plan mean anything, and does it have any teeth or force when adopted? The answer to that is a decided "Yes." To illustrate the point, we turn, again, to the Florida law:

Section 12.   Legal status of comprehensive plan.—

(1) After a comprehensive plan, or element or portion thereof, has been adopted in conformity with this act, all development undertaken by, and all actions taken in regard to development orders by governmental agencies in regard to land governed by such plan or element shall be consistent with such plan or element as adopted. All land development regulations enacted or

amended shall be consistent with the adopted comprehensive plan, or element or portion thereof.

(2) (a) After a comprehensive plan for the area, or element or portion thereof, is adopted by the governing body, no land development regulation or land development code or amendment thereto shall be adopted by the governing body until such regulation, code, or amendment has been referred to the local planning agency for review and recommendation as to the relationship of such proposal to the adopted comprehensive plan, or element or portion thereof. Said recommendation shall be made within a reasonable time but no later than two months within the time of reference. If a recommendation is not made within the time provided, then the governing body may act on the adoption.

(b) For purposes of this subsection, "land development regulations" or "regulations for the development of land" include any local government zoning, subdivision, building and construction, or other regulations controlling the development of land. The various types of local government regulations or laws dealing with the development of land within a jurisdiction may be combined in their totality in a single document known as the "land development code" of the jurisdiction.

(3) (a) A court in reviewing local governmental action or development regulations under this act may consider, inter alia, the reasonableness of the comprehensive plan, or element or elements thereof relating to the issue justiciably raised, or the appropriateness and completeness of the comprehensive plan, or element or elements thereof, in relation to the governmental action or development regulation under consideration. The court may consider the relationship of the comprehensive plan, or element or elements thereof, to the governmental action taken or the development regulation involved in litigation, but private property shall not be taken without due process of law and the payment of just compensation.

(b) It is the intent of this act that the comprehensive plan sets general guidelines and principles concerning its purposes and contents and that this act shall be construed broadly to accomplish its stated purposes and objectives.

MAKE THE PLAN A WORKING PLAN

With an enabling act such as this it is clear that the master or comprehensive plan does have the opportunity to be a meaningful and effective document. The legal status is helpful, but the important point is how the plan is supported and used by citizens, planning commission, and governing body. No decision relating to community growth, redevelopment, social improvement, or budgeting should be made without consultation with the plan and an examination of the effect the decision will have on the plan's objectives as they relate to the total community. This is not to say that the plan will be infallible or that it is rigidly cast in concrete. It does say that the plan's purpose should be to bring into focus sufficient information and data so the best possible objective value judgment can be made. Only in being used in this way by mayors, council persons, directors of public-works departments, developers, and interested citizens can master plans and planning be something more than attractive reports and interesting exercises. The understanding of this by the governing body and the public is equally the responsibility of the planning commission.

So we see that all planning commssion members should recognize that their work is really only getting off and running when the plan has been prepared. The completion of the plan is by no means the completion of the planning program. The plan must be publicized, explained, examined, and revised where necessary. It must also be kept current and not hung on the wall in the form of a beautiful colored picture, delightful to see but bearing no resemblance to the actual community unfolding outside the municipal building. It must be used in order to be effective. If it is not going to be used, it will, of course, have no effect upon the community and will be simply an academic exercise with a small degree of value in return for the investment of time and money put into it.

6. The Relationship of Zoning to Planning

Over the past several decades, zoning has become a much used word in the vocabulary of the average citizen. This does not mean, however, that the word has achieved a concensus of meaning or that the average citizen has learned to distinguish between good and bad zoning. Nor does it mean that everyone is in favor of zoning. It does mean that the course of events has led to the legal tool to help control the phenomenal growth and development that has taken place in this country. This tool is the zoning ordinance.

As more and more communities adopt new zoning ordinances and revise old ones, the responsible citizen becomes curious to learn more about the subject. Because effective zoning is dependent upon the support of informed concerned citizens, it is important to have a good understanding not only of the term but of all the ramifications of this essential element of the democratic process.

HOW IT ALL GOT STARTED

In thumbing back through the pages of time, it would probably be difficult to identify the precise point at which zoning started. It *is* known that the beginnings of zoning were quite different from the modern, sometimes overly involved, ordinances of today. It is also well established that the first zoning attempts were primarily for the purpose of preventing so-called objectionable uses from occurring in residential

71

neighborhoods. The first recorded court cases are California cases dealing with a brickyard and a hand laundry that were declared to be undesirable neighbors for homes.

As the 20th century got under way, additional experiments in the regulation of the use of structures began to appear in various parts of the country. Also, persons interested in civic improvement, architects, engineers, landscape architects, and lawyers, advanced the idea that the American city was a disgrace and needed drastic improvement that could only come from some form of governmental regulation. Attraction to this field resulted in several lawyers becoming specialists in this form of legal regulation, foremost among them Edward M. Bassett. Many credit Mr. Bassett with being the father of zoning as we know it today.

These two additional ideas (the use of buildings and civic improvement) appeared in the first comprehensive zoning ordinance in this country, an ordinance for the City of New York, in 1916. Here, for the first time in our history, a major city enacted a law regulating the use of land and buildings, the density of population, and the height and bulk of structures. Several other major zoning ordinances quickly followed in other cities, many requiring litigation and court tests. Courts' reactions to these ordinances varied; but the fundamentals of legal acceptance of zoning were established by the Supreme Court of the United States in 1926 when it refused to interfere in a case in which a state court had upheld a zoning regulation. From that point on, zoning flourished even though there continues to be judicial examination of the reasonableness of the techniques and procedures involved.

Since those early days we have been through a depression, a world war, and a population and building explosion. Community and city planning has developed as a function and a responsibility of government. Experts in the fields of sociology, economics, and geography all have repeatedly called our attention to the existing and projected population growth and the spread of urban development. Experience has shown us that, in such times as these, exploitation, self-interest, greed, and a lack of foresight are always highly evident. We have learned also that what has happened to our urban areas in the past is often inefficient, expensive, unattractive, and undesirable. We have at least learned enough to know that people, left to their own devices without self-regulation, will almost inevitably destroy the desirable features of environments, and that zoning is a necessary regulation to give order and direction to the development and redevelopment of our cities.

IF YOU'RE GOING TO DO IT, YOU OUGHT TO KNOW WHY

While many aspects of zoning are subject to a variety of interpretations, the basic concept is the exercise of the governmental power to legally regulate the use of land and the structures thereon in such a way as to protect public health, safety, and general welfare. In other words, zoning is the enactment of a law by public authority that controls and regulates private property. A more complete description of the zoning process has been given in *Local Planning Administration* (1959) as follows:

> Zoning consists of dividing the community into districts or zones and regulating within such districts the use of land and the use, heights, and area of buildings for the purpose of conserving and promoting the health, safety, morals, convenience and general welfare of the people of the community. Zoning is the instrument for giving effect to that part of the comprehensive city plan or master plan which is concerned with the private uses of and the private developments on privately owned land—as distinguished from that part which is concerned with public uses and facilities. The zoning map or zoning plan along with the regulations pertaining thereto are thus a part of the master plan—in essence the comprehensive use plan of the community—while the enactment of the zoning ordinance and its administration are the legislative and administrative acts or processes for giving effect to or carrying out this part of the comprehensive plan.

From this it can be seen that zoning is of extreme importance to existing and future development of a community. Because it does restrict private property utilization, many people resist zoning, as will be later discussed, and it could even be asked why it has spread so rapidly and grown into common acceptance in the face of this opposition. Former New Jersey Supreme Court Justice Harry Heher explained that and added to our understanding of the basic definition of the process when he said in a public address in 1956:

> Zoning is the modern response to the individual and collective needs of community life, the living together of unrelated, interdependent people, a society growing more complex as it ex-

pands. Although a concept of comparatively recent origin, zoning has its roots in basic societal necessities and pressures that from the very beginning of social life demand the accommodations of individual interests to the common good and welfare. . . .

Before any community can zone, it must have the authority to do so granted to it by the state legislature. In each of the state enabling acts, most of which are based upon the standard enabling acts prepared by the U.S. Department of Commerce in the 1920s, a statement of purposes of zoning is set forth. The ones included most commonly are:

1. To lessen congestion in the streets.
2. To secure safety from fire, panic, and other dangers.
3. To promote health, morals, or general welfare.
4. To provide adequate light and air.
5. To prevent overcrowding of land and buildings.
6. To avoid undue concentration of population.

While the language may vary and embellishments may be added from state to state, these are the fundamentals usually set forth as the objectives for zoning in any enabling act.

There are, however, other purposes that have become commonly accepted as desirable goals for zoning. For example, it is well known that zoning is the means of achieving a logical pattern of land-use developments. Without zoning, land-use development will be haphazard and hodgepodge. Through zoning, land utilization can be guided in such a way that it will make sense both economically and from a physical-design standpoint. This objective is achieved by dividing the zoning process into the formation of a zoning map and zoning ordinance text. The map sets forth zones or districts within which certain uses are permitted to occur and certain others are not. The text explains the uses permitted and defines the minimum standards for each zone and the use therein. In this way, similar and related uses can be kept together and dissimilar and unrelated uses can be separated so that they will not cause an adverse effect upon each other.

IS ZONING "UN-AMERICAN"?

There are still those who, through lack of understanding or for some personal motivation, oppose zoning as an undue infringement upon private rights. Fortunately, those who accept the legitimacy of zoning well-founded in sound planning principles are rapidly increasing. This point needs even wider discussion and public attention, for some of the most justified criticism comes from improper action taken under the name of zoning. I was once asked to take the negative side in a debate on the question "Is zoning an unconstitutional infringement of private rights?" in a Pennsylvania community in rural Bucks County. My worthy opponent for the evening was a well-meaning individual whose view-point could easily be justified as a result of his experience. He had previously lived in a community in which zoning had been subjected to a great deal of political abuse. The only zoning he knew was certainly objectionable, and, as a result, to him the entire principle was wrong. When I see a situation like this, I am reminded that the failure of individuals is often used to justify discarding the system. The world would have been in sad shape if we had decided to give up the use of ships just because the "Titanic" sank.

The secret to overcoming this is to better the system, correct mistakes, and accomplish the more universal education of our people in order to permit them to judge quality. Fundamental to this is an under-standing of the role of planning in zoning. While zoning predates planning in most communities, it has become increasingly evident that this is a case of putting the cart before the horse. Zoning based upon a well-documented land-use plan makes sense. Zoning based upon arbi-trary opinion, the pressures of vested interests, and the pet schemes of individuals acting in emergencies does not make sense.

It is the role of planning and the function of the planning commis-sion to provide a means to avoid the danger of an undue and improper discretionary approach to zoning. Whether the matter under consider-ation is a new zoning ordinance, an amendment, or a variance to stated requirements, the work of the planning agency should provide the foundation for the wisest possible decision. If the planning function has been properly followed, information is readily available to evaluate the question of the benefit to the total community and the general public welfare in every zoning question. If zoning is the legal means of regulat-ing private property to achieve orderly land-use relationships—and there is no doubt that it is—how can any new zoning ordinance even be considered unless it is founded upon the precepts of planning and supported by adequate study? I can attest to the desirability of this from the times I have appeared in court as an expert witness. Presenting information to show that the above was the foundation upon which the zoning ordinance I was defending was based was essential to winning the case and sustaining the local action.

PLANNING THE ZONING ORDINANCE

Recognizing this, the legislatures of most states have provided the means for basing zoning upon planning. Many zoning enabling acts require the planning body to act as the commission responsible for drafting a new zoning ordinance. If not actually stated, there is a strong implication in most acts that the planning commission should perform this function. In those states in which a separate zoning commission is permitted, close coordination with the existing planning commission is essential; and even in the absence of a planning commission the principles of comprehensive planning should still be applied to the formulation of the ordinance.

When a planning agency is assigned to perform this function, it has at least three responsibilities. First, it should conduct studies in order to determine the most appropriate zoning districts and regulations on a planning basis. These studies should largely follow the outline presented in the preceding chapter dealing with the master plan, particularly with regard to the elements of land use, population, transportation, and economics.

Second, the planning commission should inform the public of its activities and seek the public's views. This is done by the distribution of material and by discussion, in both formal and informal meetings. When the most satisfactory ordinance has been assembled, it must then be subjected to an official public hearing by the planning or zoning commission. The purpose of this hearing is to ensure that the opinions of the public will be heard and recorded. A good commission, however, never waits until the officially required hearing to make certain that the public understands the commissions views, and that the commissioners, in turn, understand the views of the public.

Finally, the commission advises the elected officials of its recommendations. It is the responsibility of the governing body to make final determinations and to enact the recommendations, if appropriate, into law. If the governing body opposes the recommendations, it may reject them, an action usually requiring a two-thirds vote instead of a simple majority. If, however, the proper coordination and liaison has existed between the commission and the governing body, little difficulty should be experienced. To make certain that understanding of the recommendations is achieved, the commission should provide sufficient data indicating the reasons for its conclusions in addition to the ordinance text and maps. It is also wise for the elected officials and commission to meet together several times prior to the introduction of the ordinance to jointly explore and discuss the reasons behind the proposed ordinance.

These same principles should apply in the comprehensive revision of an existing zoning ordinance. Because many ordinances were adopted prior to planning, the need for a general redrafting frequently exists. Even the best zoning ordinance needs to be subjected to re-examination and revision approximately every five years in order to make sure that it is geared to changing conditions. Here, again, the planning commission is the appropriate review agency.

ZONING BOARDS OF APPEALS (ADJUSTMENT)

Once an ordinance is adopted, a zoning board of appeals must be created. Some say that the board of appeals, inasmuch as it deals more directly with zoning, should be the agency that redrafts the ordinance. While the knowledge and experience of the members of the board of appeals should certainly be used, it is not appropriate for it to redraft the zoning ordinance. This would be comparable to asking the courts to draft the legislation they are required to sit in judgment on at a later date. It is the responsibility of the planning commission, however, to make certain that the knowledge of the members of the board of appeals is interwoven in the ordinance revision. At the same time, it is the responsibility of the members of the board of appeals to recognize their role in zoning as well as that of the members of the planning function and to cooperate in every way possible.

Far too many zoning boards have failed to recognize the relationship of zoning and planning, and some even resent that the planning commission has anything to do with zoning. The classic example of this occurred some years ago in a major New Jersey city. An old zoning ordinance was being revised: under New Jersey law, a function of the planning agency. The zoning board took offense that they were not asked to do the job and announced that they would boycott any meetings called to discuss the revision. Not satisfied with this, they even organized opposition to the suggested revision; were joined by the building inspector, a political hack; and succeeded in blocking the passage of the revision for three years, by which time all progressive changes had been withdrawn from it. It is interesting to note that in this city the members of the zoning board were paid a salary, and appointment was considered a political patronage proposition subject to all kinds of organization pressure, with a corresponding oversight of the question of individual qualifications for membership. This may help to explain the action in this case, as well as the fact that in one year in the same city, of 110 requests for variance from the ordinance requirements, 100 were granted.

Proper action by any board of adjustment is dependent upon a thorough understanding of the planning principles involved and the comprehensiveness of the zoning scheme. The zoning board has the authority to grant or recommend exceptions and variances where necessary in order to avoid hardships that would result from the strict enforcement of the ordinance. Indiscriminate variance action or the granting of special favors can eat the heart out of good zoning quicker than any other action. A variance can result in changes in characteristics that will destroy the appropriateness of good zoning requirements. Poor zoning board action and governing body support of such action is, in my opinion, the greatest cause of the starting of blight and the creation of slum conditions that we have today.

I recall, for example, a community in which I had worked to prepare a master plan. I found that one of the most obvious needs of the community was for an attractive, substantial commercial area. At the same time, the desirable characteristics of open space and other suburban amenities needed to be preserved. A special highway commercial area was devised with rather elaborate standards as to lot coverage, setbacks, parking, and landscaping. During the adoption of the zoning ordinance, an individual with special interests challenged the ordinance in court. After a most extended and expensive litigation, the ordinance and its principles were upheld in their entirety as being a part of a comprehensive plan.

The community then looked forward to a brighter future with desirable commercial ratables. Alas and alack, the zoning board, which evidently thought that all of the advance preparation was simply an academic exercise, failed to keep this in mind. Within one month after the final settlement of the case, a large store decided to locate in the area. The developers, of course, wanted to squeeze the most out of the land that they possibly could. Consequently, they applied to the zoning board for a variance, pleading hardship, although economic hardship is not a legitimate consideration. Within 15 minutes, the board had granted them variances from seven of the basic requirements, any one of which alone would have destroyed the meaning of the ordinance. Fortunately, there is a happy ending to this story. The planning commission immediately protested, gained the support of the governing body and the people of the community, and had the variance revoked. Regrettably, there are many similar occurrences each day that are not prevented and therefore go their merry way undermining good zoning and planning.

AMENDMENTS, ENFORCEMENT, AND ADMINISTRATION

In the case of amendments to the zoning ordinance, the planning commission is usually used as a referral agency. This means that when an amendment is contemplated it must be referred to them for report and recommendation prior to its adoption by the governing body. This is logical, of course, in the proper planning-zoning relationship. Improper amendments can weaken or destroy good zoning and in the long run can destroy the prospects for good planning proposals. The final decision as to whether to amend the zoning ordinance should be based upon what it will do to the master plan of the community. The planning body should be in a position to make this determination and to clearly state the reasons for its conclusions and recommendations. Many states require that, if the report is unfavorable, the amendment can be adopted only by a larger-than-majority vote of the governing body.

In reviewing an amendment, the planning comission should be certain to give the most careful attention to the following:

1. The effect of the proposed amendment on the comprehensive planning of the entire municipality.

2. The changes in community characteristics that may take place because of the projected change.

3. The relative effectiveness or ineffectiveness of the present wording of the ordinance, and whether a justification for change exists because of either special reasons or a change in conditions.

4. Whether the amendment is designed to correct an improper situation or would result merely in the granting of special privileges.

If these factors are carefully considered and sufficient data are available for evaluation, a sound recommendation will result. In some cases, it may be necessary for special studies and surveys to be made in order to obtain enough information to answer the questions. Where this is true, the commission should not hesitate to investigate, making certain that professional technical assistance is used wherever possible. In the case of a major amendment, a good technique for ensuring that the above points are thoroughly explored is to require an environmental impact assessment of the project proposed.

The final factor to be considered in the relationship of planning and zoning is that of enforcement and administration. To some, it may seem that, inasmuch as these are not the responsibility of the planning commission and not directly connected with planning as such, they are of questionable importance and not worthy of mention. To me, nothing could be further from the truth. I have seen many good zoning ordinances and the corresponding planning schemes ruined by lax enforcement and uninformed, inept administration. Because enforcement and administration are day-to-day affairs, they can have far-reaching effects on the preservation of sound principles. Thus, the planning agency should be well aware of their importance, informed of their prosecution, and insistent upon their efficiency. In most communities the basic job of enforcement falls upon the zoning officer, who in many cases is also the building inspector. This public official can, by the performance of his or her duties, seriously affect the success or failure of the zoning ordinance. An ill-formed official with little understanding of the principles of zoning cannot be expected to be alert to the importance of his or her opinions or be expected to apprise the planning commission of current problems in zoning. In today's complicated urban structure, part-time enforcement is not enough.

Even full-time enforcement by an uninformed or disinterested individual can be not only inadequate but also destructive. I experienced this in one municipality in which the building inspector, again, was given the responsibility to act as zoning officer. As it turned out, he was opposed to the whole idea of zoning. He said nothing publicly about his feeling but granted permits in conflict with the ordinance. The planning commission was lax in follow-up, and it was not until a year had passed and a great deal of harm had been done to the intent of the ordinance that his peccadillos were discovered and halted.

In recent years, in addition to the zoning officer who is responsible for issuing permits, many communities have created the office of zoning examiner or zoning hearing officer in order to speed up the process of resolving some of the more routine zoning questions and to relieve the board of adjustment of some of its work load. This officer has been given the authority to act on conditional uses and special exceptions that are spelled out in detail in the ordinance along with administrative standards. He or she also may be authorized to rule on requests for variance from the lot or area requirements where there are exceptional physical features involved that would make strict compliance with the ordinance impossible. While the use of a hearing officer can be helpful administratively, here too it is of utmost importance that the holder of the office be well versed in the planning process and that any action taken not be detrimental to the intent and purpose of the master plan.

NEW TRENDS IN ZONING TECHNIQUES

There are constant efforts to develop new ideas in land-use control and growth management, all of which must be founded on zoning or at least the theory of governmental police power. These include cluster or density zoning, which allows deviation from fixed lot size based upon an overall density control factor; performance zoning, which evaluates a development plan on density, open space provided, impervious surfaces created, and the overall impact on the area; transfer of development rights, whereby each parcel in a district is assigned a number of development rights based upon planning considerations, such rights being transferable between properties in that district or other districts similarly classified; and planned unit development zoning, whereby, in essence, a "master plan" of integrated development of a large parcel or parcels of land can supercede the zoning standards that would normally apply based on the zoning map. All of these are important and have contributed greatly to providing additional flexibility and design freedom to zoning. With this flexibility, however, has come an even greater need for correlation with comprehensive planning. The planned unit development technique, for example, is really the application of planning principles in order to achieve a more cohesive and imaginative development pattern than could result from traditional zoning. In most cases, communities using this technique in their zoning require all such applications to be submitted to the planning commission and approved by them before any other processing can take place.

As time goes on and our communities continue to grow and face additional problems from development—or don't grow and must find means to stablilize and redevelop—still more new techniques and practices will be initiated and tried. The one thing of which we can be sure is that government has and will continue to have a great deal to say about how land is used. In order to understand this, it might be well to remember the basic stimulants that have led and will continue to lead to the furtherance of zoning. A prime stimulant is that of necessity. As communities are spread upon the countryside, we have encountered the necessity of regulating one of our most precious assets, our land. We cannot face the future of becoming more urbanized without recognizing that there will be an increasing stimulant for the imposition of governmental regulation upon the utilization of private property. While this certainly poses a potential danger, it also offers possible salvation for our future communities. The question of *which* it shall be is largely in the hands of the citizen. If we understand zoning and recognize the importance of being a vital part of it, the end result will be beneficial and desirable. If we fail to take an interest or to become concerned, the necessity of regulation will continue and the gap will be filled by a higher level of government with an increasing loss of freedom of choice on the part of the individual. This is of such vital importance that it should be repeated over and over.

It also should be repeated that zoning is a tool of planning and will be as strong and effective as its planning base. This is true not only in the case of the original zoning ordinance but also in revisions, amendments, and variances. Any zoning change can effect the planning of a community, and close cooperation must be maintained between planning and those responsible for zoning.

7. The Regulation of Land Subdivision

Some years ago, as a planning consultant on the East Coast, one of my job requirements was to spend many hours behind the wheel of a car, traveling hundreds of miles throughout the urbanizing countryside attending meetings and working client communities. In this going from place to place, I found myself continually struck by the effects of urban sprawl as it devoured the landscape. There were two aspects that particularly stand out in my mind. The first is what I call the rape of the roadside—the mute testimony to man's greed and shortsightedness that lines so many miles of spoiled highway frontage. That, however, is another story to be told in much greater detail at another time. The second is the way in which the subdivision of land into building lots and parcels has played leapfrog over the countryside, seemingly caring little where it makes the next leap. In many cases, there is little rhyme or reason to the areas developed. Residential communities, shopping areas, and industrial tracts are all carved out of the first field available that offers the least line of resistance. Any resemblance to a pattern or plan for general development appears to be coincidental rather than intentional. All that is required to engender a subdivision is a nearby concentration of population.

As development scatters over an area, seeking the cheapest and most easily developable land, it brings with it a great many problems. Each house must somehow have a water supply, a means of sewage, garbage, and trash disposal, schools for children, and protection against fire and other dangers. Stores and industry likewise sometimes create more problems than advantages in traffic generation, parking, and servicing. Streets and roads, many times with little thought given to their layout and design, add miles that must be maintained, resurfaced, plowed, and drained. Frequently there is little relationship between subdivisions, and streets dead-end into yet untrampled fields or hillsides. What lies on the other side of the hill or across the field is given little thought.

THE PIECES SHOULD FIT TOGETHER

The unbridled tendency of development to follow the line of least resistance, like the flow of molten lava but without the same continuity, is one of the most outstanding sources of planning and development problems today. Far too little attention is given to the importance of orderly relationships between areas of growth. Nor is the total solution to be found in requiring the installation of utilities and services in individual subdivisions. I once had some experience with a semi-rural community of some 30 square miles that had 11 separate and disjointed residential subdivisions of over 300 homes each. In their wisdom, the town officials thought that by requiring the installation of package sewerage plants they would avoid a major headache. While they avoided the problem of overflowing septic tanks, they completely overlooked a number of perhaps even more complicating factors. For example, there was no common design control of the systems. As a result, as the area filled in and a public sewer system became desirable, not one of the individual systems had been designed so that it could be tied to any other. Each of the 11 systems had its own disposal unit. As the developers pulled out, the municipality found itself responsible for the maintenance of each unit, which required trained technicians. In the long run, the costs of correction were staggering; in essence, the residents of the community provided a subsidy for the exploiting developers. This is to say nothing of the expense of providing schools, school buses, street maintenance, and all of the other services to this disjointed municipality.

In observing this and the literally thousands of similar situations across the nation, I wonder if we really realize the importance of our control of the subdivision of land. While frequently given little attention, it is one of the most important facets of community planning and development. As a field of 10 or 100 acres is carved up, a piece of the future community is molded. Each lot, each building, each street is like a building block that will determine the characteristics, the problems, and the potential of tomorrow's community. In an era of unprecedented growth, this is the way we are building the cities of tomorrow. Even in our older areas, the subdivision of large lots, estates, and golf courses can seriously affect the master plan of the city and the patterns of development. Subdivision, defined as the division of land into lots, tracts, or parcels for the sale and development thereof, is the means by which we are fitting together the pieces of the jigsaw puzzle that will be the future community.

ENACTMENT OF CONTROLS: THE FIRST STEP

The control and regulation of the subdivision of land is usually accomplished by the enactment of a subdivision ordinance or the adoption of a resolution setting forth standards. In most instances, while final approval may be in the hands of the governing body, the administration of subdivision regulations is the responsibility of the planning commission. The commission may simply act as a review agency, checking the subdivision in accordance with the regulations, examining its relationship to the master plan, and passing on its recommendations to the governing body for action. In some states, the planning commission may be authorized not only to review but actually to approve or disapprove subdivision plats. In many states having large unincorporated areas, subdivision control may be vested in county planning boards, a situation that is becoming more prevalent as urban growth spills outside of the corporate boundaries of cities and towns. Some states, such as Pennsylvania, have even gone so far as to permit county planning agencies to impose regulations on an incorporated area when the city itself has failed to act after a stated period of time.

Conversely, an increasing number of state enabling acts grant cities what is known as "extra-territorial" authority to regulate land development on their fringes. Thus, a city may extend its subdivision control a specified distance, usually three or five miles, from any point of its corporate boundary. The purpose of this is to assure the municipality the opportunity of staging its utility services in land that it probably can expect to annex in the future and to avoid the intensification of development of the open countryside to the point that later public services would be difficult, if not impossible, to provide. The proper and careful use of this extra-territorial authority is a most important tool to a city, particularly one that forms the single central core for a surrounding unincorporated territory of a rural or semi-rural nature. This again illustrates the importance of recognizing that land subdivision regulations and controls are a vital part of the planning process.

Subdivision guidance and control can make or break a master plan, particularly in an open community. The need for municipal services will be directly related to the subdivision activity in the community. The master plan should include a careful study of all open areas and should anticipate their ultimate development in the most appropriate use of land. The effectuation of the land-use plan then becomes a joint venture between zoning and subdivision control. In areas where expansion is yet to occur, the master plan can anticipate the need for school sites, major streets, parks, playgrounds, and drainage right-of-way. Many states permit either the reservation or acquisition of these areas as the land is subdivided. Some enabling acts even provide that a fee may be required in lieu of land dedication to ensure that adequate recreation facilities are provided within the community. Certain developers, recognizing the value of their investment, are not only providing school sites but are also building the schools.

When the Levitt Corporation built its third Levittown, now known as Willingboro, New Jersey, not only was the land for schools provided but the first high school, junior high, and several elementary schools were constructed by the developer.

CONTROLS MAKE DOLLARS AND SENSE

Proper anticipation of development and preparation for it through master planning and subdivision control can save the community thousands of dollars. My firm worked in any number of communities where the fact that a new major street had been proposed in advance resulted in the dedication of the needed right-of-way as the land adjacent to the alignment was developed. Communities have also corrected existing inadequacies in street rights-of-way by requiring additional width in accordance with the master plan as subdivision took place on each side. On the other hand, some communities have attempted to go through the motions of subdivision control without a master plan (a practice permitted in some states) or seemingly have forgotten that they have a plan and have treated subdivision as a separate, independent operation.

In either case the effectiveness of subdivision control has been serious-ly limited. Without reference to a well-prepared plan, the approval of subdivision plats becomes nothing more than an exercise of collective thinking, limited in scope, discretionary in requirements, and totally devoid of comprehensive considerations.

Illustrative is the case of the community that failed to take into account an overall plan of streets and roads in its subdivision control. A large triangular area of several hundred acres of the community was eventually developed in five separate subdivisions. Not only was no provision made for a much-needed collector street in the area, but the growth generated far more traffic than the inadequate existing streets in the area could handle. In this case, the former mistake could not be corrected at all, due to the placement of the houses, and the later error was an extremely expensive one to correct. Worse, the new homes had been permitted to build so close to the existing inadequate roadway that its ultimately necessary widening destroyed their desirable char-acteristics and led to the spread of cheapening and ratable-destroying uses.

Subdivision regulations should clearly establish the rules under which the development of land will be permitted. Careful thought should be given to the preparation of such regulations, and they should be phrased in as clear and concise terms as possible. An understandable procedure for application, processing, and approval should be pro-vided.

Advice and assistance on how to develop a good set of subdivision controls are available from many sources. There are suggestions and model ordinances that can be obtained from state, county, and regional planning agencies, as well as from national groups. The latter ones include, among others, the American Planning Association and the National Institute of Municipal Attorneys. Many state municipal leagues provide excellent materials and assistance to their members. One of the best publications available, not only on subdivision but also on the complete process of planning and zoning, is that issued (1977) by the Utah League of Cities and Towns, entitled *Planning and Zoning Ad-ministration in Utah.*

A word of caution is in order, however. Even the Utah League staff will tell you that, while many model ordinances exist, the regulations should be specifically designed for the individual community and tai-lored to its special and specific problems.

PUTTING THE ORDINANCE TOGETHER AND MAKING IT WORK

A good subdivision ordinance usually contains a set of definitions, procedures for filing applications, descriptions of the methods of processing, approval procedures, design standards, and provisions for general administration. The definitions section sets forth what is meant by subdivision and may exempt a minor subdivision of a limited number of lots from the full approval process. The procedural section sets the time of filing, states the required forms and materials, and outlines the steps that have to be taken. The design section deals with the necessity of installing streets, curbs, gutters, sidewalks, street signs, and trees and establishes minimum standards for each. The administration section provides for appeals from decisions, establishes final approval authority, and outlines the manner of conducting public hearings, if they are required. Of utmost importance to subdivision control is the provision of a carefully drafted set of application forms for use both by the applicant and, as a checklist, by the planning commission. Usually a performance bond or guarantee is required of the subdivider to insure the installation of required utilities and facilities.

Regardless of the quality of the ordinance, the success of subdivision control and regulation will be dependent upon the care with which the ordinance is administered. A planning commission cannot take this assignment lightly. Each subdivision plat should be carefully reviewed by the entire commission. Members should personally view the area under question. This should be done as a special trip, even if they drive by the area every day. Somehow it will appear different to them if they look at it with the map of the projected subdivision before them. In addition, each application should be carefully checked as to form and the provision of adequate information. The effect on the master plan should be examined and discussed. The zoning requirements for the area should be checked to be sure they are being met. Other agencies of the community should be informed and consulted, particularly the school board, the board of health, and the engineering department.

The commission should not hesitate to make suggestions for improvement of the subdivision design. In many cases, careful review can result in an improved design that will save money for both the developer and the municipality. My firm worked out a system in some of our client communities in which each subdivision plat was referred to us for review and, if desirable, redesign. A fee was assessed by the municipality against the developer for this service so that it was not a cost to the community. Not only were the communities saved thousands of dollars by the reduction of street lengths and resultant maintenance costs, but the developers on numerous occasions stated their gratitude for improvements in the design and character of the area.

Just as is the case with zoning, recent trends in subdivision control techniques have been toward providing greater flexibility of design and the means of interrelating diverse, but compatible, development. As new zoning tools such as planned unit development and cluster development have come more into use, a broadening of the opportunities to shape community form through subdivision review and approval has taken place. To do so requires a very close coordination between the provisions of the zoning and subdivision ordinances. Some people believe that the time has come to consolidate land-use and land-development regulations into one composite ordinance. This would incorporate in one document all of the regulations pertaining to the development of land, whether it be use, lot sizes, design, or the provision of utilities and services. Whether or not this is done, it is becoming increasingly obvious that the division of land that shapes the urban form and its utilization must be closely correlated and both must be based firmly upon the total comprehensive planning process.

A word should be said about the importance of subdivision controls as applied in land development of other than single-family residential. Frequently industrial, commercial, and multi-family uses necessitate the subdivision or re-subdivision of land to achieve the desired site. This is especially true in the use of the planned unit development concept and in the assembly of parcels for redevelopment in some of the older areas. A good set of subdivision regulations requiring extensive design and site plan review can ensure an attractive and efficient result. Such things as traffic circulation, ingress and egress controls, landscaping, and open-space development can be part of the overall approval package and can make the difference between an outstanding project and another drab scar on the horizon. Many subdivision ordinances require this type of design review before approval can be granted.

Of equal importance is the understanding of the value of dedication of land and easements through subdivision review. Several years ago, the courts looked rather unfavorably on requiring any outright dedication of land from a developer, whether for parks, schools, or any other public purpose. This attitude has changed decidedly as the problems of municipal financing have increased. Dedications of land for parks, passive open space, schools, bike trails, and safe access for children over and under major traffic arteries are now commonplace. As the energy crunch continues, the availability of public lands for bicycles, walking, and even mopeds will remain a major concern. Often this can be tied to other vital aspects of development controls—stream right-of-way protection, flood control, and drainage. A wooded trail along a drainage easement that allows safe pedestrian and nonautomotive vehicle movement can be a priceless asset to both the community and the subdivision.

What all this adds up to is that subdivision control is an indispensable tool of community planning. This is true whether you think of the need for guiding the future development of your community as a "growth management plan" or still utilize the separate but related functions of zoning and subdivision controls. Just as zoning shapes and maintains the community character, subdivision controls shape the development pattern of individual areas and consequently the whole community. Subdividing patterns will determine the adequacy and efficiency of future streets, utilities, schools, police and fire protection, and garbage collection, as well as the economic benefit or liability of any particular subdivision to the overall governmental unit. Good subdivision planning and controls are the ways we can permit development while making certain that, when development occurs, it will fit into the overall scheme of the master plan with the least detriment and the maximum benefit to the community.

8. The Capital Improvements Program

Americans are cost-conscious and, in most cases, conservative about expenditures in everything but government. More and more of our total income is taken to run the business of government, each year seeing a continuation of rising budgets and expanding operations. Somehow we seem to have become conditioned to expect huge amounts of public funds to be expended and to believe that little if anything can be done about it. While it may be necessary to accept the idea that little can be done about the continual rise of funds required to provide the demanded services, a great deal can be done about seeing that the money spent for public improvements is well spent. (California voters, by enacting "Proposition 13" in 1978, severely restricted their state's governmental spending by limiting the tax that can be placed on real estate. Perhaps I am wrong to say "little can be done about the continual rise of funds," but I am not sure that "Proposition 13" was the right approach.) We can do a great deal to assure the public that its money is buying the most needed project and that the results will make good sense. This can be accomplished on a municipal level through the use of the capital improvements program.

PROGRAM PUBLIC FUNDS IN ADVANCE

Every day in this country, literally millions of dollars are expended in connection with public improvements, and by public improvements is meant any service or facility provided by a government and paid for with public funds. The construction and maintenance of water systems, sewer systems, streets, sidewalks, municipal buildings, parks, and fire stations are among the items considered in the capital improvements program. Schools, while usually considered separately, are a vital part of the community's capital expenditure program, particularly during a time of growth and expansion. All of these facilities and services are being planned, built, and maintained by our municipal governments each hour of the working day.

The provision of these services and facilities is essential to our way of life. In fact, the real justification for municipal government lies in its ability to provide protection, services, and facilities better and more economically than we ourselves can on an individual basis. Yet probably 75 to 90 percent of the funds spent for public facilities are spent on projects that have not been subjected to a careful analysis, justifying their need and making certain they are an integral part of a comprehensive long-range plan. Instead, they are approached on a piecemeal basis as the need arises and the pressure gets great enough to force action. Action may also wait for the development of an emergency, such as the failure of a well at the pumping station, the collapse of a rotten storage tank, or even the overcrowding of houses on too-small lots and the consequent oozing of effluent into the streets.

One of the most important purposes of planning is to anticipate the needs of people for public improvements and to provide a sensible program for meeting those needs. This is the function of the capital improvements program phase of master planning. The program is usually supplemented by the development of a capital improvements budget. The program itself is a summary of the needs of the community in terms of public improvements, the estimated costs of these improvements, and the development of logical priorities for their provision. The needs are determined by the master plan and the work of the planning commission in analyzing land-use and population trends, economic pressures, and general development potentials in terms of the financial capacity of the governmental unit to provide the service. The priority of need can be determined only after a careful study of the master plan and a detailed analysis of the opinions of the various municipal departments as to their needs. Each improvement should be justified in relation to all others. The more a project is needed by the total population, and not by just one or two groups, the higher its rating should be on the priority list. The cost of the total program must be related to the economic base of the community and what it can afford at a given time.

DON'T GET CARRIED AWAY ON THE
"RATABLE BANDWAGON"

As general obligation bonds usually are issued to provide the funds for capital improvements, and as most of the money to repay these bonds comes from the ad valorem or real estate property tax, all proposals must be carefully scrutinized as to how they will affect and relate to the tax assessment base. All states, through one form or another, control municipal borrowing, either by establishing a bonded indebtedness limit or by state approval of municipal budgets. Thus, a city may not indiscriminately borrow money or exceed the amount set by the state, except in the case of an emergency that threatens health and safety. The debt ceiling and amounts that have been borrowed and not repaid must be taken into account in preparing the budget for any future capital expenditures. As net taxable valuation rises through economic growth, and as past obligations are paid off, the municipality's borrowing capacity increases. This system has been one of the major causes of governmental units closing their eyes to sound planning principles and jumping on the "ratable bandwagon," allowing poor development that promises to increase the tax base.

The development of a capital improvements program, if it is to be successful, must be a cooperative endeavor. Each and every operating department of the community must be willing to understand and support the program. To a large measure, the basic capital needs are determined by the information compiled from the individual departments. This is usually done by the use of forms and questionnaires submitted by the planning commission or its staff to each department head. The department head then indicates the department's capabilities, its shortcomings, anticipated needs for new services, and necessary replacements for old facilities, with cost estimates where appropriate. When this information is returned to the planning commission, it is carefully studied and evaluated in terms of the overall community. A complete list of the needs for efficient service over a five- or six-year period, with approximate costs, is then prepared as the program of capital improvements, and recommended priorities are assigned each item. A capital improvements section of the community budget is then adopted by the governing body for the first year to take care of the financing of that portion of the projected improvements that the community can afford at the time. (Some selected pages from the capital improvements budget of Albuquerque are included in "Appendix B" as illustrations.)

Many states require the preparation and adoption of a capital budget by statute. This is frequently overlooked, particularly in the smaller cities. It is part of the planning function to insist that careful capital improvements programming and budgeting are worked out and that they have the support of the people.

Where the capital improvements program is practiced, it is found to be an extremely valuable tool. City managers have long been advocates of the idea of capital budgeting. Many of them feel not only that it is the desired way of properly programming an improvement but also that it is the best way of avoiding undue pressure from vested interest groups for a pet project.

SUCCESSFUL CAPITAL PROGRAMMING MEANS PEOPLE INVOLVEMENT

When I served as city manager of Albuquerque, I found the capital improvement program to be one of our most important undertakings. Each year it was approached with a sense of concern over the way in which the needs outweighed the available finances and concern over how to make certain that each dollar brought the most service to the total population. It is equally true that some of the most controversial discussions with department heads and pressure groups in the city took place over the final decisions made. Many cities have found a well-prepared program equally useful, and such places as Cincinnati (long noted for its advance planning), Dallas, Phoenix, and Hartford have used capital budgeting as a most successful way of anticipating new expenditures and bond issues well in advance of emergency needs. By so doing, a city administration can prepare studies and illustrate the necessity for each project to the people.

This cannot be overemphasized. Without the understanding and support of the taxpayers and voters, no capital improvement planning is going to reach fruition. In Albuquerque, each time we were successful in a bond issue, the large share of the credit could be given to a representative, aggressive citizen committee organized to study, support, and publicize the needs of the city. Philadelphia and other places have used the media—especially radio spot announcements—to inform citizens of the details of proposals and to explain just why each is needed. The places that continue to have successful bond issue votes in spite of the rising resistance to increased governmental spending have all pursued effective public information programs such as this.

LARGE OR SMALL CITIES, THE IDEA WORKS

Lest it be assumed that the value of such a program is limited to the larger cities, let me emphasize that such is not the case. No community should operate without a carefully thought out capital improvements program. The smaller city or village may only be worrying about the provision of a few new sidewalks or the paving of a few streets, but wise programming, based upon the master plan, can be extremely beneficial. Just take the example of the community that has an effective planning commission and approaches its problems of growth seriously. The citizens may suspect that they will soon reach a point of growth at which their present waterworks will be inadequate, but they aren't quite sure when that point will be reached. They start a master plan study, which shows that regional pressures and past trends indicate a potential for 3,000 more people within the next five years. The land-use map and traffic studies show not only that this growth is likely but also that there is an area of the community that is ripe for new subdivision. The services needed to provide adequately for the new people can then be calculated. It is seen that the water plant needs rebuilding and that new service lines are a must if the area is to prosper. Through careful study and cooperation with the water department, the planning board schedules the items in the capital improvements program, and the financing is provided in the budget at an early date.

Compare this situation with that of the community that couldn't be bothered with all the fuss. They just left things to chance. If a street light burned out, it was replaced. After all, it is easier to spend folks' money if there is an emergency, and there is really less pressure than if you explain to them a need in advance. It also merits noting that it is easier to pass out political favors if there is not too much on paper about what ought to be done. This community proceeded on its merry way, meeting emergencies as they arose, and even then on a stop-gap or piece-meal basis. Of course, they never really improved; in fact, they even went downhill and were always over their heads in debt. They also found that some of the better industry passed them by, but after all, they weren't wasting any money on this planning foolishness. In case this strikes you as funny, think about it carefully. It could be your community. I have seen a good many places just like it.

Capital works programming can succeed and can be a valuable effectuating tool of sound planning. It is frequently resented and resisted. Sometimes, because of petty jealousy, an individual department head who feels that cooperative capital works programming will interfere with his or her own empire building will attempt to discredit or delay it. Sometimes elected politicians will try to discredit the procedure, knowing that their porkbarrel method of dispensing services as favors may be interfered with. Regardless of the reason for objection, the well-versed planning commission member and interested citizen will realize that sound capital improvements programming and capital budgeting are the keys to long-range economic stability within the framework of the master plan.

9. The Care and Feeding of Planning Professionals

Whether you are a member of a planning commission, a citizen group leader, or just a person interested in what is going to happen to your town, it is desirable for you to know a little about who is going to be parceling out planning advice in your community. This means, or should mean, the planning professional, the person who delves into data collection and research, comes up with analyses, and makes recommendations to the planning commission and the policymakers. Just what kind of people are these and how do they come by the title of professional planner? Doesn't everybody plan? Aren't my ideas of what our community should be 10 years from now just as good as anyone else's? The answer to the last question is probably "Yes"—if we all had the kind of training that teaches us to examine thoroughly and think comprehensively in terms of total societal concepts and if we could really think objectively instead of personally about where we live.

The planning professional should be a generalist who has knowledge of sociology, ecology, economics, geology, engineering, law, and public administration and at least some understanding of physical design. The effective planner must also have an understanding of people and how to deal with them and have the patience to accept frustration. Above all else, while retaining professional principles, the planner must become a skilled student of politics but not a politician. This is the kind of awesome charge those of us in planning education are facing today—to provide this type of background and knowledge in the brief period of our relationship with students.

AND THE LORD SAID,"LET THERE BE PLANNERS"

The function and the profession of planning have expanded rapidly over the past several decades. Future prospects appear to indicate an even further expansion of both government- and citizen-activated community planning. This planning will no longer be confined to land use, public facilities, and physical growth but will include dealing with social problems, programs for community services, citizen organization, and other "software"matters. All of these are things that will affect our lives in one way or another; and, while the planners are not decisionmakers, the work they do will influence the decisions that will be made. For that reason, the citizen should know who the planners are, the training and experience they have had, and the nature of their role in shaping policy.

The first planners in this country were persons who, in a position of leadership, had vision and foresight. Paterson, New Jersey, for example, points with pride to the fact that Alexander Hamilton provided it with its first plan for development. Thomas Jefferson had an intense interest in architecture and city planning. The founders of Washington, D.C., even went so far as to engage a specialist, Major L'Enfant, to lay out the circles and radials now famous in that city, if not effective in today's traffic. Many of our existing cities can thank their early pioneers for the few spots of green and open areas that remain, such as the park squares in Philadelphia. While some professionals in allied fields began to appear on the planning scene in the late 19th and early 20th centuries, it was not until the public works program of the Depression years that the specialized practice of the profession emerged.

With the planning and programming of public works for relief purposes came the realization that they should be related to comprehensive planning. As a result, state planning boards were formed and enabling legislation for local planning passed; architects, engineers, and landscape architects became involved in land planning. It was soon recognized that physical planning alone was not enough, and economists and sociologists were brought into the field to perform essential research. As the merits of the idea of comprehensive—that is, physical, social, and economic—planning became obvious and the demand for planning increased, it was only logical that a separate profession should evolve and that educational institutions should initiate specialized training.

The number of institutions so doing also has experienced a phenomenal growth in recent years. Upon departing from an architectural background and venturing into the field of planning in 1947, I found no more than five such programs and all at the graduate level. The total student enrollment could not possibly have exceeded 100. At present, planning, or some related area of specialization, is taught in organized schools or departments at some 100 colleges and universities, at both the undergraduate and graduate levels. More schools embark on such programs every year.

LOOK, MA, I'M A PROFESSIONAL

Today, a well-schooled planner is given courses in planning principles and concepts, methods and techniques or research and analysis, social problems, citizen activation, housing, environmental concerns, law, public administration, economics and governmental finance, and physical design. He or she may be basically schooled in a physical science or in a social science and may begin specialization at the graduate level or may enter one of several undergraduate planning schools right out of high school. While there are those who insist that persons skilled in one of several allied fields, such as architecture or engineering, are qualified professional planners, it is becoming more and more generally accepted that comprehensive land-use planning is a separate process requiring, for maximum competence, special training as well as specialized experience.

As the planning profession evolved and grew in numbers, those interested in the field banded together in a formal professional organization. Thus, the American Institute of Planners came into being more than 50 years ago. This organization now has a national headquarters in Washington, D.C., and individual chapters all over the country. Strict membership requirements have been established, and the organization is dedicated to the improvement of professional standards and practice. A code of ethics for planners has been administered by the AIP, and standards for the education of planners, together with a list of colleges and universities meeting these standards, have been prepared. A planning agency or an individual can obtain general information on planning and planners from the Institute. (As of October 1978, AIP and

ASPO merged into the American Planning Association, maintaining offices in both Washington and Chicago.)

The planning commission embarking on the job of planning for an area very quickly finds that professional services in some form are not only desirable but are usually essential. The typical commission is comprised of persons who, though interested and perhaps partially skilled in planning, lack a complete knowledge of planning techniques. In addition, members are, in many cases, active civic leaders with their own professions to practice. The amount of time most can devote to the development of plans for the community is limited. Few, if any, technical surveys and studies can be accomplished by two- or three-hour meetings once or twice a month. It thus becomes obvious that if planning is to be meaningful, someone skilled in its practice and with time to devote to its prosecution must be found. This means the employment of a professional planner. Professional services can be obtained on one of two bases—either by employing a full-time resident staff or by hiring a consulting firm.

HELP WANTED—FULL- OR PART-TIME

The first of these, staff planning services, is the method of creating within the local government a technical staff, employed by the city and responsible to the planning commission (or responsible to the chief administrative officer but working with the commission). The administrative organization of staff planners varies, of course, from one municipality to another. The staff may consist of one trained planner, as in the case of small cities, or may number several planners, researchers, graphic artists, and secretaries, as in the larger cities and large-scale planning operations. Many of the larger cities have an annual planning budget of several hundred thousand dollars and a planning staff that varies between 75 and 100 persons. The majority of local planning offices, however, are the small, one- or two-person operations, usually consisting of a planning director, an assistant, and a secretary.

In a small staff operation the selection of personnel is extremely important. The planner must have a well-rounded background. He or she may be working on a technical study of traffic circulation one minute and be expected to deal with a complicated zoning problem the next. The individual must be skilled in technical matters, be a public relations expert and an administrator, and at the same time be able to deal with political intrigue and changes in the power structure of the community. The success or failure of planning as a process can be dependent upon the planner's ability and personality.

It is of utmost importance to the program to make sure that the personnel obtained are the best for the job. Many planning programs, off to a flying start amid local enthusiasm, have been set back or completely killed by selection of the wrong personnel. I well remember an illustration of this in a New York community. There, after years of effort, a planning program was initiated with great fanfare and public expectation. For over a year, the program developed nicely: a master plan and a downtown rebuilding scheme were formulated with the assistance of consultants. The community, wanting to ensure continuity, decided to engage a staff planner. The salary scale was comparatively low, to keep it in line with established governmental salaries, and the community was a challenging one for any planner. After advertising, some six or eight applicants were interviewed and several were offered the job, only to turn it down. Finally, for fear that a long delay would result in the loss of the appropriated funds, the decision was made to accept an applicant with less than the desired ability and experience. As a result, within six months the community's planning and urban renewal program was in a state of complete confusion because of the lack of experienced and mature direction. There developed a serious question of whether planning as a function was to be abandoned, yet the community continued to need planning even more than before. While a staff operation can be effective and desirable, the importance of careful selection and the paying of a salary sufficient to attract top-flight personnel cannot be overstressed.

The second method of obtaining professional planning services is that of engaging a consulting organization in the planning field. Consultants are available for advising as to program and review of activity or to provide actual staff services. In many communities, a combination of staff and consulting services is utilized. Here the consultant provides review of the staff work and lends experience and know-how, or undertakes special technical studies, including the development of the master plan, to supplement the work of the staff. Again, the selection of an individual or firm is extremely important.

THERE IS SOME GOOD AND SOME BAD IN ALL OF US

There are advantages and disadvantages in both methods of providing services. The success of any planning operation will, in large measure, be dependent upon the individuals involved, and it is well to be aware of all significant factors. The staff planning office offers the opportunity for the planning function to have a direct relationship with the local administration. The planner becomes a part of this administration. A planner living in the community has the advantage of intimate familiarity with the area and its problems. He or she can see the pressure spots and evaluate the matters most demanding of attention. A staff program also provides continuity and puts planning on a day-to-day basis. The planning commission has technical advice immediately available, and a direct contact with the people of the area can be maintained.

The disadvantages of staff operation frequently stem from the very things that appear to offer advantages. The local planner often gets overrun with day-to-day housekeeping chores and has little time left for real planning. The planner is sometimes too readily available to all the pressure groups and runs the danger of becoming emotionally involved, either on a friendship or interest basis. Objectivity can be lost by familiarity. In addition, it is far easier for a local staff employee to be subjected to political pressure and to weaken, understandably, when job security is at stake. At the same time, it is difficult to find personnel for the staff operation who have the broad experience required to ground the planning operation on sound principles. Infrequent is the one planner who has sufficient skills in all required technical fields, public speaking, public relations, and political organization to provide all that is needed for a successful local program.

The consulting system, on the other hand, has the advantage of overcoming many of these objections. A well-qualified firm can offer broad training and experience. Members of the firm usually are schooled in varying disciplines and have worked in many different communities. They can draw from this experience, saving time and, in many cases, avoiding damaging mistakes. Consultants are free to work without interference from local pressure or vested interests. Being independent of the community, they can be more objective, and, at the same time, their opinions can carry more weight. Consulting services can be obtained by communities feeling that they cannot yet afford the budget required for a staff operation. In many cases, two or more communities within an area can combine and, using the same consultant, obtain staff services for the expenditure of far less money than required for individual staffs or even a combined staff.

The most frequently mentioned disadvantage of the consulting system is the danger of one-shot, package planning. This certainly should be avoided; if the program is carefully undertaken, it can be. In addition, the consultant may be unable to become as familiar with the community as a staff planner. He or she can prepare technically competent studies that overlook matters of immediate local concern. The work can also be made meaningless by the failure of the planning agency to become an integral part of the project. There is, too, the difficulty of keeping the planning commission and the public well informed as each part of the program unfolds.

Having been on both sides of the fence (public staff planner and private consultant), I cannot help but have mixed emotions, which I believe allow me to see the advantages and disadvantages of each method rather objectively. As a former president of the American Society of Consulting Planners, I can strongly endorse the multi-facet expertise of the private practitioner; and as a former planning director, I can say with assurance that the continuity of staff planning is vital and beneficial. My conclusion bears out the idea that even if you have a good staff, there are times when a consulting firm can be invaluable.

The desired program for any given community is, of course, the program that best serves the community's needs and suits its characteristics. Whether this is staff alone, consultant alone, or a combination of the two, there will be advantages and there will be pitfalls. Good planning commission members recognize this, as they realize the importance of the individual characteristics of the planning personnel. The key to the success of any planning program is the care with which the personnel, whether it be staff or consulting firm, is selected. Good commission members also recognize that no professional can solve all of the problems alone. They must have the understanding and support of the local people. Local policy and ultimate effectuation will always be the responsibility of the planning commission and elected officials. In most cases, the results of the planning program will be determined by the combined abilities of the professional planner and the lay members of the planning agency—no more, no less.

THE DAY OF JUDGMENT MUST COME FOR ALL

As there are going to be more planning commissions and more planning professionals involved with all of us in the future, it is reasonable to reflect on a few guidelines that might be helpful to the citizen in evaluating and dealing with both. Some could be questions to which answers should be known; others are caveats about which we need to be aware. They include, but are not necessarily limited to, the following:

1. Who is considered to be the client? Is it the mayor, the council, the political structure, the developers, or the people in general?

2. Are the professionals and the commission members keenly aware of the importance of citizen involvement and citizen opinion? Do they welcome participation and comments from citizen organizations and individuals?

3. Can the commission members or the professional be counted on to be objective, impartial, and reasonable? Is there any strong personal motivation, such as real estate investment or furtherance of other business interest, that may cloud thinking and create a conflict?

4. What is the professional's background in education and experience? How did the individual fare in any other communities in which he or she worked? What kind of formal training has the person in planning?

5. Are the commission members and the professionals socially aware? How do they deal with minority problems, the question of adequate housing, and the need for increasing economic opportunities for all? Can they work with people of all ethnic and economic groups in a fair and considerate way?

6. What is the administrative structure for planning? Are the professionals given a realistic opportunity for the expression of ideas and the offering of advice, or are they expected to be "rubber stamps" for politically expedient action? Does the

mayor or chief executive have a planning attitude and insist that the planning department receive the necessary cooperation from other departments and agencies?

7. Is the planning director truly a professional with the administrative capabilities to run an efficient department or is he or she there as a strictly political appointee who must be very careful not to "rock the boat?"

8. Are the staff members competent? Are they permitted free expression of ideas and opinions and encouraged to further their own education and knowledge as well as develop new concepts and techniques?

9. Is there frequent turnover of personnel and have highly regarded professionals left for other more satisfying and better-paying positions? Is meritorious service rewarded by advancement and assignment of additional responsibility?

10. What was the last proposal of a major consequence to emanate from the planning professional or the department? How was its presentation handled, and what was the result in action or lack thereof?

11. Does the public in general know of the work of the planning department? What is their opinion of it? Have the professionals gained the respect of the citizens, the planning commission, and the governing body, or are they just there so we can say there is a planning function?

WE ARE ALL IN THIS TOGETHER

A satisfactory answer to all of these questions is needed if there is to be a meaningful planning process. Planning is a function of collective society working together to better the environment; the professional is only the catalyst. No professionals who feel that they are planning *for* people instead of *with* people are going to be very effective; nor are they professionals in the true sense of the word. At the same time, all of us should remember that the planner is a human being, too, with feelings and pride. Regardless of how we may disagree with his or her ideas, each is also entitled to the same kind of courteous treatment, objective consideration, and fair play as we expect they will provide us. We should keep in mind that we are all in this together: only by working together as those who share common concerns can we expect to make things better. The job of your professional planner is to help you, me, and others to make this possible.

10. Planning and the School Board

One of the most perplexing mysteries in modern society is our persistence in the separation of community planning and school planning. Yet not only are they undertaken completely separately; in most places they are approached competitively and, in truth, compete for the same diminishing tax dollar. Planning for community development and planning for schools have so much in common that merely to say so seems redundant. It is not even the chicken and the egg question of which came first: the interelation is so great that they should be planned for in concert—collectively and cooperatively. It is only in this way that the school system can adequately serve the area of its jurisdiction and that the community or communities involved can relate their growth policies to the' educational system. It is only in this way that both public community needs and school needs can share equitably in the division of the tax dollar.

AS THE TWIG IS BENT, SO SHALL IT GROW

The provision of adequate school buildings on well-located sites is one of the most important community responsibilites. Each area must provide the needed facilities and personnel to school the youngsters who live in the jurisdiction or who are yet to come. The school board has little to say about the rate of growth of any area, yet it is obligated by law to provide an adequate public education system. With the rising costs of construction, and of operation after construction, we find that larger and larger percentages of the local tax dollar are going into school purposes. In some cases, from 75 to 85 percent of total tax funds necessary for local public purposes are used for schools. The anticipation of this need, and the means of providing some measure of control for orderly growth in order to avoid runaway costs for education, can only be achieved by the cooperative endeavor of the school board and the planning board.

With our changing social structure, the revitalization of inner-city core areas, and the continuing shortage of energy and resources, this coordination becomes not just important but essential. Because of the decisions of the courts on desegregation, emphasis has had to shift from planning the neighborhood school to which children could walk to a much more comprehensive planning of the physical educational plant for the entire district. This means not only developing and maintaining reliable demographic statistics on existing and future school population but also being keenly aware of shifting trends of residents and changes in land use. This is further complicated by the results of urban renewal and attempts at rebuilding and revitalizing inner-city neighborhoods. Some places have found that older schools with declining population, and once thought to be obsolete, are valuable assets as new life is breathed into an urban fringe and as busing of students has become a way of life.

Another matter of mutual concern in our changing social structure illustrates the need for effective coordination between community planning and school planning: the problem resulting from expanding metropolitan areas with multi-jurisdictions. As the suburbs bulged and schools became overcrowded, the lack of pupils in innner-city schools afforded the opportunity for economies of which advantage has not been taken. It is foolish for one school located near a municipal boundary line to have insufficient pupils to justify its remaining open while another school four blocks away in another jurisdiction is so crowded it is on double sessions. This occurs in many of our metropolitan regions, however. At this point it becomes necessary to comment on the sociological inequities of political and educational systems. While we profess to believe in democratic principles and justice, it takes no great insight to recognize that bigotry still exists and is a fundamental cause of educational imbalances between the inner-city and the suburbs. Efforts in the past to overcome this have not been notably successful, but recent court decisions regarding desegregation and the necessity for all governments to provide a full range of housing types and opportunities, as well as the inappropriateness of supporting education from local real estate taxes, portend that change is in the wind. These factors and many other telling arguments give great credence to the thought that school and city/suburban/rural planning should go hand in hand in preparations for the future.

DON'T TREAD ON ME (OR MY KINGDOM)!

The organization of the school board, however, results in built-in potential conflicts to coordinated planning. In our determination to keep school systems free of politics, we have done everything we could to create the impression that good school administration necessitates complete autonomy and independence, not just in administration but also in school planning. School boards, whether elected or appointed, have often been led to believe that no one else should even consider the question of the location of a school or of its effect on the community. With the expansion of comprehensive community planning, however, planning commissions are finding that the provision and location of schools are factors that cannot be skimmed over or left to a single agency. No master plan is complete unless the school question has been properly related to the general community, its needs, and its potential.

This was something that a planning commission chairman with whom I was involved had not learned. Etched in my memory is the day I attended a public hearing on a zoning amendment held by the commission chaired by this gentleman. The request was for a rezoning to permit a large apartment complex in what was a single-family area. The neighbors were up in arms and out in force. Their cause was expressed by a spokesperson who emphasized the problem of impacting and overcrowding that would occur on the neighborhood school if this project received approval. The chairman began loudly banging his gavel, saying. "You are out of order. School matters have no place in this hearing. The planning commission has nothing to do with schools. That's the school board's problem." It goes without saying that the project was approved; and it can be added that, with outstanding, intelligent friends like this chairman, the community did not need any enemies.

Experience has shown me that rare indeed is the school board that does not appear to resent the action of community planning related to schools. (A noteworthy exception to this is the situation in Portland, Oregon. There, the school board has charged its director of planning with coordinating school planning with community planning.) There appears to be a feeling that only those elected or appointed to the school board can or should even be concerned about the effect that a million-dollar yearly budget and a multi-million dollar capital expenditure program for new schools can have on the total community plan. I have seen school boards refuse to permit the planning commission access to enrollment figures and in other ways seek to obstruct the formulation of a master plan. This in spite of the fact that most state planning enabling acts specifically indicate that the expenditure of public funds for any such matter is an element of legitimate concern to planning. This attitude has even resulted in litigation between school boards and planning commissions in extreme cases of uncooperativeness. Fortunately, such cases are rare, and resentment seems most often to arise from simple misunderstanding.

Nevertheless, I have never been able to understand why any feeling of resentment should exist. The responsibility of any board, commission, or agency of a public nature is to the people of a community: its goal is the betterment of the total community. If planning can be used as a means of better locating schools or guiding growth so that orderly tax rates can be maintained, why does it matter whether there is only one agency or 16 worrying about the problem? The planning commission, of course, has no right to attempt to tell the school board or the educators how to run the schools or what to teach, but it can and should provide wise counsel on the location and priority of construction of buildings, the coordination of school sites with the community recreation program, and the fiscal abilities of the municipality within the forseeable future.

WHY ARE WE TOO SOON OLD AND TOO LATE SMART?

Comprehensive planning is important to the school problem today more than ever before. As communities spread out in the horizontal sprawl so characteristic of present growth, school systems are swamped with bigger and bigger headaches. Proper advance site selection can often save thousands of dollars not only in land acquisition but in reduction in length or even the elimination of unnecessary bus routes. Zoning and subdivision control are the only two legal means of regulating land development. If these are coordinated with existing school capacities and plans for future expansion, a sensible and economical approach can frequently be evolved that will save dollars and headaches. Zoning, when based upon a sound plan, can regulate densities of population, which, in turn, create demands for schools. While the capacities of school systems cannot be the sole basis for zoning, they can be given weighted consideration in the development of zoning standards. Subdivision design and control can relate community growth to a planned core with easy-to-reach, safe, and convenient school locations at the center. Frequently, needed land for school buildings or school and recreation expansion can be obtained at little or no cost to the community by the adept handling of a major subdivision.

Through cooperative endeavor directed toward comprehensiveness, communities and their school boards can avoid being placed in the situation that I found a suburban township in several years ago. This municipality had been right in the path of the urban expansion steamroller. While this fact had been known for some time, neither the governing body nor the school board had done much about it. The elected officials felt that planning was unnecessary, until conditions got completely out of hand and there was no choice but to institute a planning board and enact a zoning ordinance. By then the population had increased, in a six-year period, from around 3,000 to 16,000. There were only five small elementary schools; all other students were transported to a nearby municipality. Every grade was on double sessions, and in order to correct this within five years, 143 new classrooms had to be built at a cost of from $25,000 to $30,000 per classroom. This is to say nothing of the additional costs for teachers, transportation, and administration. A little advance planning, a touch of school board cooperation, and a bit of firmness in principles on the part of the elected officials would have done much to offset this staggering prospect.

In view of this kind of tremendous capital outlay, it can be seen that there is still another reason for planning and school coordination. We have seen how sensible planning requires the weighing of each capital expenditure against the total community need. While school needs are vital, the well-rounded community is the one that knows when it can afford schools and when it will be doing more for all concerned by providing other public facilities. In many cases, proper capital expenditure planning does not mean the rejection of school facilities but instead means making certain that such expenditures are properly timed to fit the community's ability to pay. It is an unwise community that blindly ties up its entire bonding capacity in schools because of a fear that they will be needed while letting raw sewage run in the streets for the lack of an adequate treatment plant. In the long run, such objectionable conditions will discourage the attractive, ratable-producing growth that would produce sufficient revenues to provide good schools—not to mention good streets, water service, sewers, and parks. Schools, while absolutely vital, are only a part of the total community.

LET'S TAKE AN ASPIRIN—MAYBE IT WILL GO AWAY

Although I am a firm believer in adequate educational facilities and am always available to vote for an increased salary scale for teachers, particularly since becoming a college professor, I cannot help feeling that the community that stabs out frantically at the school problem, ignoring all else, is like an individual treating a persistent headache. The pain is frequently only symptomatic of a much more dangerous ill. The pain can be dulled, but the basic disease goes on unchecked. I always get this feeling when I see school boards appoint citizen study committees who go out and count all the new kids and then extend a straight-line projection to show skyrocketing enrollments for the future—all with little or no consideration of the overall conditions in the community that may affect the rate of growth. While these committees are no doubt well-meaning and sincere, if they are going to work in a vacuum, ignoring comprehensive community problems, they might as well stay home and watch television.

The planning commission that works in a vacuum can, of course, be offered the same warning. No planning agency has the right to ignore the school board or the school problem; nor has it any right to assume a dictatorial attitude. Planning can provide information on the total community frequently unavailable to the school board; and, in reverse, no planning commission can possibly know as much about the school problem as do the school administrators and the members of the school board. The sensible and effective role for each is one of complete cooperation and coordination. The planning commission should provide the basis for relating school needs and projects to the master plan.

The investigations of land use, population, traffic, and the economic base of the community should enable it to provide valuable counsel in school planning. The school board should be able to see the value of an overall master plan and envision the easier task ahead for it if school plans are part of a general community scheme.

DON'T CONFUSE ME WITH FACTS—MY MIND'S ALL MADE UP

One word of caution to planning commissions: no planning agency has the right by its mere existence to pass upon or review school board plans. A commission unwilling to assume its responsiblity to plan forfeits its coordinating position, in my opinion. The purpose of relating school planning to comprehensive community planning is to allow it to be placed in the proper perspective in terms of careful studies and investigations—not to be judged by mere uninformed opinion. The only planning commission in a position to evaluate realistically is that one which has at its disposal all of the information needed for an intelligent decision.

Community planning and school planning are important partners in community building. Each has its place, with the responsibility for overall coordination belonging to the planning commission. Neither will be successful without the other. The real element of concern is to make certain that both recognize that they have a common goal, the achievement of which should be uppermost in their minds—that is, making our community a better and more efficient place in which to live. Whether lines of prerogative are slightly crossed in achieving that goal is certainly immaterial.

One final comment regarding the relationship of planning and the schools: school boards and their employees can be of great service to the future of our communities. Because good school planning is dependent upon good master planning, school people should insist upon first-rate community planning efforts. If a serious deficiency in planning exists, the public should be informed. One of our most crying needs is for citizens who know what planning is and who can tell the difference between good and bad planning. More discussion of the subject and courses related to city planning, regional planning, and community development should be instituted in our elementary and high schools. When I once suggested this to a well-meaning curriculum planner, she informed me that this was well taken care of already: after all, each civics and social study class spent one week studying the government of the town.

I don't mean this kind of glossing over of the basic problem. Let's teach our children that the physical community can be planned, that good planning is comprehensive, long-range thinking, and that it will make their cities finer, more efficient, and more economical. They are smart enough to learn this quickly and then see that poor planning and the lack of planning are stamped just that. They can then build better communities, with better schools, and ultimately a stronger, better nation.

11. Planning and Other Community Development Functions

Few other problems of our times have been more discussed than urban ills and the plight of our cities. Through the years, as society has become more complex, it has become increasingly apparent that all is not well with cities, old or new. Better means for carrying out plans for more livable environments have been constantly sought; but too often the process of comprehensive planning, inasmuch as it is advisory in nature, has been unable to stem the tide of decay or to assure an improving situation without policy support and pragmatic effectuation tools beyond land-use controls. While courts have generally given greater weight to community interests and acted favorably on progressive zoning techniques to a helpful extent, this alone cannot change the facade of our urban areas.

The evidence of past mistakes that exists in the form of inadequate streets, rundown business districts, pollution, decaying and deteriorating homes, and violence and crime is all too clear. Major portions of larger cities have become identified as obsolete, depressing, and costly slums. Nor is this confined to one municipal unit in major metropolitan areas. Blight has a way of ignoring political boundaries and spreading across the land like the relentless flow of lava. Even in the newer suburban communities and the less densely developed urban areas, blocks of shacks, hovels, or outmoded structures and facilities not only are found in existence but also, unfortunately, are being created every day. Thus, we no longer have just an inner-city problem but find ourselves having to deal with a metropolitan and even regionally common malady.

In recognition of this as well as of the fundamental obsolescence of the inner-city and the need for improved housing for low-income families, the federal government, through various programs since the 1930s, has attempted to provide encouragement and direction. Some of its attempts have failed miserably, either from bureaucratic insistence upon unworkable standardization or because of local ineptness and mismanagement. Examples include "Operation Breakthrough," the "Model Cities" program, the New Communities Act, and the "General Neighborhood Renewal" program. Many of these were short-lived due to their lack of success or the constant changing of administrative policy. The longest lasting governmental effort, and one that is still with us in some form, has been that of slum clearance and urban renewal.

Since the early public housing legislation of the '30s, emphasis has been on the need for rehousing those caught in the "urban trap" who live in blight and decay and who are unable to improve their lot without assistance from society. This concept has survived, although it has been broadened and adjusted by Congressional acts over the past three decades to include not only slum clearance but urban redevelopment and urban renewal as well. With the advent of "New Federalism" and the move to reduce specific categorical funding and institute forms of revenue sharing, urban renewal was merged into the Housing and Community Development block grant program. Continuance of existing projects was provided for, but new attempts at urban renewal are required to be part of the overall allocation of funds through special revenue sharing or block grant allocation of the Community Development program.

URBAN RENEWAL OR "URBAN REMOVAL"?

As we have had urban redevelopment and urban renewal for some 30 years, and they will continue to be referred to and used in some form, it seems appropriate to review how they worked and will work and their relationship to comprehensive planning. Assuming there was in existence appropriate state enabling legislation, the local governing body started urban renewal by the passage of an ordinance creating a local public agency (LPA), outlining its purpose and granting authority to clear blighted areas, acquire and sell property, use eminent domain where required, and "renew" selected areas through private enterprise investment or public housing. The LPA could be the governing body if that agency so chose, a housing authority, or a separate urban renewal authority. The majority of the communities have opted for the separate agency, which upon creation assumed a semi-autonomous (in some cases almost a dictatorial) stature. In a number of instances, this led to conflict between comprehensive planning and pragmatic project planning and execution. While almost all state acts required coordination between planning and urban renewal, placing the responsibility for surveying an area and certifying it as "blighted" with the planning commission, LPA's invariably resented the necessity for revealing plans in advance and relating proposed re-use of land to a comprehensive plan.

After several troublesome projects resulting from lack of integration and/or bad management that left many cleared areas unused except for parking, Congress tried to overcome some of the problems via the Federal Housing Act of 1954. It was here that the first federal funding for comprehensive community planning was provided and the requirement for a workable program for community improvement (WPCI) instituted.

This latter consisted primarily of a statement of "good intention" on the part of the community showing that it had or was preparing a master plan, administrative coordination, reasonable financing arrangements, necessary codes and ordinances, an active citizen participation program, and a real desire to improve itself. The theory and purpose of this WPCI was most praiseworthy, but like many other well-intended federal stipulations, in the majority of cases only lip service was paid to it by those who were supposed to administer it at the federal level and by local officials.

As the late Dennis O'Harrow, the highly respected former director of the American Society of Planning Officials (now APA), once said, "What this country's planning and renewal needs is fewer 'workable programs' and more programs that work." Personally, I continue to be both perturbed and disturbed by the naive idea held by Congress and federal bureaucrats that desirable and high-sounding "guidelines" or requirements can be effectively enforced. We all know what effect a simple telephone call from a member of Congress—one whose home territory has suffered strict imposition of these standards—can have when placed to the head of a department charged with administering the standards. All of us in the consumer public are naive if we continue to accept this snake oil.

MEANWHILE BACK AT BULLDOZER HEADQUARTERS

Meanwhile back at the office of the local urban renewal authority (LPA), probably they had been going merrily on their way designating project areas and filing loan and grant applications, the first step in the process. Once an area had been certified as blighted and the Department of Housing and Urban Development had processed their loan and grant application, they were in the position to acquire property by either negotiation or condemnation. This done, they could clear the property and sell it to private developers. Once sold, development was required to conform to a re-use plan that had been approved by local agencies and HUD and that was specified in the project execution application, the final phase of submittal to HUD before actual work could begin. Throughout all of this, comprehensive planning and renewal were theoretically cooperative partners in reshaping the urban scene into a more desirable, livable environment. Regrettably, such was not always the case.

Similar to the difficulties that developed between long-range planning and short-range zoning of the past, problems in cooperation between public housing agencies, local public agencies, and planning seem to be difficult to avoid. Public housing policies and any program of community revitalization should be an integral part of any comprehensive planning process. Achieving this coordination seems to be as difficult as finding a cure for the common cold. Part of this stems from the amount of autonomy given to housing and renewal authorities and the retention of the idea that planning and the work of the planning commission is *only* advisory. It is easy for an agency authorized to take action to feel that any time taken to relate that action to planning research and study as well as citizen involvement in objective determination of goals is a waste of time.

While this view is myopic and sometimes fatal to a housing or renewal program, the fact that it has been permitted to exist can be credited both to the failure of federal and state legislation to recognize a proper role for coordinated planning and to human frailty at the local level. Never have I been able to understand that destructive tendency of men and women theoretically working for the same ends who nevertheless fail to cooperate with each other, building up instead a resentment against the imagined interference of an advisory agency. As planning is more public-participation-oriented, it would be easy to say that the base of this is partly an unwillingness to bother with an informed public rather than just ego-centered parochialism. Any intelligent member of any other public agency, whether it be housing authority, urban renewal authority, library board, or school board, should realize that a close relationship between any one of their special projects and the comprehensive planning process is desirable. The more successful the individual project, the more credit will be due the sponsoring agency. Yet many communities are sitting with half-finished or abandoned urban renewal projects, newly created slums in housing projects or other mislocated public facilities, largely resulting from petty squabling among local agencies all supposedly existing to service the same public.

LOOKS LIKE IT WON'T GO AWAY

Both urban renewal and public housing will continue for years even though there may be new nomenclature. As of this writing, both have been made part of the Community Development block grant program. Through the Community Development Act, several programs relating to community development have been consolidated into this approach to special revenue sharing. Funds are allocated to a local area based upon past spending and need and are then parceled out to allowable or eligible projects by local officials working with a representative citizen's advisory group (CAG). The members of CAG are supposed to represent all geographic, economic, ethnic, and social facets of the community. Again, this program starts out with commendable sounding intentions—involving citizens and letting them and the local officials decide where and how the available funds will be spent with the fewest possible federal strings attached. It will be interesting to see if it works this way and how long it will continue to do so.

It is important to emphasize again the need for coordination. Assuming that CDA continues to be the source for funding for redevelopment, public facilities, clearance, housing rehabilitation, and code-enforcement programs, the question arises as to how this will be related to the comprehensive planning process. We have seen how writing a requirement into a federal act for coordination and compliance with a sound planning base has the same guarantee of success as writing the U.S.S.R. a polite note and asking them to please stay out of Cuban affairs. The planning commission should play a vital role in the entire CDA process, and all projects approved, whether they be for "hardware" or "software" programs, should be clearly a part of a comprehensive policies or traditional master plan.

To do otherwise is to allow spotty, piecemeal, and often pork-barreling projects or programs to continue. Here is another place that the planning-commission-conceived and local-governing-body-effectuated capital improvements program should play an important role. Any CDA funds allocated to physical facilities should reflect and be in harmony with detailed and informative planning studies that were the basis for the adopted capital improvement programs.

Many other individual local government functions concerned with community development and their relationship to planning could be discussed in the same detail here. These would include codes and code enforcement (many communities have now placed these in their planning or community development department), social welfare programs other than housing, cultural endeavors and maintenance, fiscal management, etc. Rather than do so, let me repeat that only through an understanding that well-functioning comprehensive planning is the hallmark of any successful business administration can effective, economical municipal management be achieved. Coordination and cooperation among various individual or independent functions is recognized as essential if the entire operation is to succeed—or survive. Good, efficient government is just as dependent upon good business administration as is IBM, General Motors, or AT&T. An effective, dedicated mayor or council member recognizes this and will give top priority to see that all community-development-related functions are based upon and coordinated with the comprehensive planning process.

THE POTENTIAL VALUE OF ENVIRONMENTAL IMPACT STATEMENTS

Before leaving the subject of coordination, we should spend some time discussing another means of making planning effective and even more people-oriented. This is the environmental impact statement (EIS), which is much bandied about but little understood. Simply stated, an EIS is a means of saying, "O.K., so you are planning a project. Now tell us all about it, and, while you are doing that, show us just what effect it will have on the environment and/or the community." If really carried to its fullest potential, this is a very powerful tool for effective planning, community-development-related coordination, and successful citizen involvement.

As early as 20 years ago, some of us in the planning consulting field were urging our client communities to abandon rigid, traditional zoning classifications and instead reduce the number of zones or districts but allow certain more intense uses in specified areas based upon their impact. In 1958, I recommended just such an ordinance to Chesterfield Township, a semi-rural farming community in New Jersey. There was to be only one zone—residential/agricultural—and all other uses were to be subjected to submittal of a special application, public discussion and hearing, and an analysis of their impact on the immediate neighborhood, the surrounding area, and the entire community. The Chesterfield officials, including their 82-year-old township attorney liked the idea and adopted the ordinance. Unfortunately, one landowner who just didn't like the prospect of any zoning took it all the way to the New Jersey Supreme Court. I now tell my classes that one of the things of which I am most proud in my career is the fact that I wrote an ordinance that was based upon the now very acceptable principle of determination of allowance by impact on environment and the general area, and it was the only zoning ordinance to ever be declared illegal and unconstitutional by a unanimous vote of that court.

Granted the present EIS has come a long way from the original attempts at impact zoning, the idea is the same. Any major project today, particularly if federal funding is involved, can be subjected to such an impact analysis prior to the granting of approval, and such analysis is often required. Analysis provides the planning commission with a good opportunity to relate to a master plan and to take full advantage of the coordination of planning. For illustration, let us assume that the agency responsible for potable water production and delivery is planning a major new filtration facility. In the old days of "business as usual," they probably wouldn't have even bothered to consult with the planning commission other than cursorily. Now federal funding is involved and an EIS is mandatory. While federal laws do not say that the planning commission is to be sole judge and jury on the EIS, the commission certainly can use the fact that submittal is required to exercise its proper role of coordinator and involver of people. There is no reason that the commission can't be the agency responsible for seeing that an objective, impartial EIS is prepared or at least have the organization preparing it responsible to it rather than the proposer agency, which obviously has a vested interest.

Such an EIS would provide a thorough analysis of the impact of the facility on water resources, water quality, land use, traffic, community or neighborhood character, open space, wildlife habitat, the capital improvements program and budget, and the fiscal ramifications for the municipality as well as the taxpayers and water users. In general, the question of what this will do to our ecology and environment would be answered. By seeking a review of the EIS by other affected agencies, the planning commission not only fulfills its role as a coordinating agency but also enhances this role in the eyes of others, thus furthering the possibility of truly successful comprehensive planning. By insisting on open meetings while the EIS is being discussed and by promoting public meetings and hearings on the project, the commission can involve more of the public and encourage citizen participation, again strengthening the planning process.

This same approach can be used by the planning commission in reviewing a request for rezoning to allow a more intensive type of use. A developer proposing a change to allow an apartment complex in what is now a zone restricted to single-family units can be required to underwrite the cost of an impartial EIS. A real estate broker seeking a change to allow land to be used for a shopping center or an industrial park should expect to follow the same procedure. The advocate of a major planned unit development can and should be asked to present a thorough analysis showing similar information. Almost any major project can be analyzed better by the developer or agency being required to have prepared and submit an EIS.

It is hoped that it is unnecessary to emphasize the fact that the value of an EIS is dependent on its being done independently and not by the proposing agency or individual. Either the planning department staff or a consulting firm responsible only to the planning commission should be used. The costs for this can be appropriately assessed to the proposer, and many communities do so. This is done in some cases by obtaining an estimate of the costs and requiring that sufficient funds be deposited in escrow by the advocate to insure payment upon completion. The idea of the EIS and the appropriate method of its handling are all important points that should be remembered in considering the tools for effective planning and the involvement of concerned citizens.

More and more we hear reference to the idea that planning is, or should be, total involvement of all of us in community development. The idea of citizen involvement, the trademark of community development professionals, is essential to the planning process in a democratic society. The Housing and Community Development Act of 1974 and subsequent amendments and the advent of the environmental impact statement concept are two excellent means for comprehensive planning and citizen action for planned change (community development) to be melded together as never before. How successful we are in doing this will have great bearing on our environment and the livableness of our communities in the future.

12. The Citizen and Planning Action

Many people, whether they are members of planning commissions or just interested citizens, have a sincere desire to get more out of planning. They want to understand it and to find out how it can help their community. Where no planning commission exists, this interest is frequently in how to get others interested and in how to get started. Even if there is a planning commission, the individual members or an interested citizen may justifiably feel that more should be done or that things should be done better. There may be a real need to secure better understanding and wider support. All of these things are important to a successful planning program. Far too many established commissions fail to have sufficient energy or curiosity to seek continually to improve themselves and their program. It is up to the interested individual to make sure that this does not happen or that planning is not delayed because of a lagging program. The truth is that each and every citizen has a responsibility to see that the community is doing the best that can possibly be done to shape its future. Unfortunately, many of us choose to forget or to ignore this simple fact.

KNOWING WHAT'S HAPPENING MEANS THAT WE CARE

When a commission exists, we can nevertheless ill-afford to sit back and relax assuming that everything is being well cared for. Though most of the members may be conscientious people—and many commissions *are* doing a good job in the interest of all of us—still we need to be concerned about their work and the quality of the planning they are doing. We should not permit ourselves to be lulled into a false sense of security by the mere existence of an agency for planning, for its program may be less than adequate for the needs of the area. It is one thing to have the machinery technically established and something else to be sure that it is functioning well and doing the best job that can be done.

Far too many myopic or ill-motivated politicians, when pressured by citizen demands to initiate planning action they did not support, have made planning ineffective by simply "going through the motions." They kill effective action by appointing the politically faithful, or they try to starve programs to death through lack of funding. I have seen such people anticipate a strong demand for planning they considered undesirable and quickly move to block any hope of good results by creating and/or supporting sham programs that they call planning. I know of an entire county that is being sold short by just such a move right now. What its officials are passing off as planning has no more resemblance to true planning for the common good than a peanut has to the Rocky Mountains. The general public, because it does not know any better or does not care enough, accepts this and, in the long run, will pay for it.

Any of us who is the least bit interested should know whether or not there is a master plan and, if there is, what its proposals are and what is being done about them. Is the plan being used to review propositions put forward by various departments of the administration, by council, and by developers? Is it truly a blueprint for building a future community? Is it truly being followed? How current is it in terms of the changing conditions of the national, state, and local trends and other forces that may affect it? These are but a few of the areas about which we all should make sure we are aware.

To better gauge the quality of the planning being done or to assist in organizing new activity, a great deal of help is readily available to assist individuals or groups. Educational materials can be obtained from many sources, both on a national and local level. As previously mentioned, the American Planning Association, with offices in Chicago and Washington, is an excellent source. Its membership is open to any interested person as well as to local officials, commission members, and professionals. Members receive monthly publications as well as information on additional publications and services available. The Urban Land Institute in Washington, while somewhat developer-oriented, publishes excellent informative documents on trends, standards, and specific problemsolving.

HELP NEARER TO HOME SHOULD NOT BE OVERLOOKED

The states and counties are not to be overlooked as sources of informa-tion. Most states and many counties have well-staffed planning depart-ments and agencies that have as a major function the preparation of educational materials, helpful statistical information, and professional assistance to local communities. For material on how to get started in planning, the job of the commission, and general information on zoning, subdivision controls, capital improvements, and just about anything else anyone could want to know about planning, the best publication is *Planning and Zoning Administration in Utah,* published in 1977 by the Utah League of Cities and Towns. Its value will be apparent to anyone concerned about planning, regardless of state of residence. State governmental agencies, as well as such associations as the Utah League, can usually provide both resources assistance and a good list of information sources.

The counties are good places to turn in many states. California counties long have been leaders in planning activity, as have several Maryland counties near Washington, D.C., Westchester County in New York, and Bucks County in Pennsylvania; all have established reputa-tions not only for their innovative action but also for their excellent publications. Note should be taken also of the many meetings and conferences held by these and other agencies. As planning has moved to the forefront in the minds of people and in government functions, more and more organized discussions on the subject are being conducted. These are not only very informative, but they offer as well marvelous opportunities to gather useful printed matter. Commission members and all of the rest of us should try to attend as many of these as possible. It is only by being knowledgeable and well informed that we as citizens are going to be able to contribute to good planning or objectively evaluate what is being done.

THE COMMUNITY RELATIONS PROBLEM IN PLANNING

Even though we have talked a great deal about information, materials, and knowledge, there are those who have said that community planning or development action is about 2 percent technical knowledge and 98 percent public or community relations. Even though this certainly is not entirely true of good planning, it is true that the success of any planning program is greatly dependent on the nature of community relations. Many of the elements of a master plan are recommendatory in nature. Even those proposals that can be enacted into legal tools, such as the land-use plan through the zoning ordinance, must be understood and supported or they will never get past the idea stage. In a democratic society, there is no stronger deterrent to the enactment of any proposition, regardless of its merit, than a well-organized, vociferous group of objectors whose ringleaders have thinly veiled motivations for wanting to see the proposal killed. The only solution to this problem in planning is to have people dedicated to the practice of good community relations and to informing as many citizens as possible of the merits of planning proposals.

No community should undertake planning until it knows what planning is. This may seem like a hard and unnecessary statement, but I have become firmly convinced that it is necessary not only that it be said but that it be often repeated. Let me emphasize that in a different way by repeating that unless there is a *planning attitude* in the community on the part of the elected officials and those who elect them, planning will solve no problems, save no money, and be of little value in any other way. Frankly, I think it is time professional planners, planning commission members, interested citizen groups—all of us—began shouting this from the rooftops and stopped letting this inescapable truth be swept under the rug or hidden in the closet.

The community that simply goes through the motions of the master planning process with little knowledge of what is involved is doing itself, as well as planning, a disservice. I was informed in one locality that no one would ever get planning started again, as they had tried it once and it had failed. Mind you, now, the statement was that *it* had failed, not that the *community* had failed. An investigation disclosed two very interesting facts. First, the thing called planning had consisted of a political, inept commission that had hired a nearby and handy fringe operator who claimed to be a planner. No effort was made to find out about planning or to engage in a community relations program. The so-called master plan consisted of a poorly prepared zoning map and a few proposals for new streets and roads. In this case, it was actually a good thing the public had risen up against it.

The second discovery was even more interesting. It seems that the mayor at the time of the preparation of this plan had been completely opposed to planning as a hindrance to his political patronage system. A local civic group had steamed up a demand for a planning commission and crammed it down the governing body's throat. The mayor had then carefully set about the premeditated murder of planning by making certain that all of the wrong things were done. The resultant revolt proved just how successful he had been. At last report, the mayor was still very happily enthroned in an ever-growing political kingdom and was very profitably selling crackerbox houses on inadequate lots as a sideline.

While this case is a study of purposeful disruption, there are many · communities that innocently fall victim to the same fate. These are the ones in which planning suddenly catches on as a good thing to do but about which absolutely nothing is known. This eventuality is frequently activated in this day of federal aid by the knowledge that the neighboring community has obtained some of that "free money" available for planning assistance. Naturally, the innocents don't want to be left out. No thought is given to the meaning of the process, what is involved in it, or the responsibility that goes with the opportunities available through planning. These are things to worry about later.

I have a vivid recollection of one municipality whose officials approached our consulting firm in just this frame of mind. In spite of all I could say, they were determined to get on the gravy train without even reading the timetable to know where it went. They applied for aid and were accepted by a state agency that for one reason or another had no time to ascertain the preparedness of the community before federal aid was granted. The results were predictable but sad. As soon as planning got beyond the basic data collection stage and into policymaking and decisionmaking, the local officials began to say that they had no idea that this type of thing was involved. Reports were unread, and, by the later part of the project, five meetings were called before a quorum of the planning commission could be assembled even to discuss the master plan proposals. Needless to say, little was accomplished by this planning program. Here again, if more people had been informed, and if even a few had understood the process, the story could have been very different.

IT'S NOT MUCH OF A PARTY IF NOBODY COMES

An informed public is essential to the organization of planning, as well as to the effectuation and activation of plans. Any type of planning activity attempted in a vacuum will in all probability fail. A well-informed citizen or commission member is aware of this and is ever alert to avoid the obstacles presented by an uninformed citizenry. In many instances, the advice of an experienced professional planner can be of great assistance in making certain that community relations are well organized. At the same time, it should be remembered that the responsibility of community relations cannot simply be passed over to the professional. His or her job is to render technical advice, not to relieve local officials of their obligations.

In any community relations activity, whether it be selling the idea of a planning commission or putting across recommendations for zoning changes, there are a number of things that should be kept in mind. The first principle is that the more citizens who can be made to understand the broad concepts and purposes of what is being attempted, the more likely is the chance of success. Far too many communities leave informing the public to chance or ignore it entirely under the mistaken theory that there will be less trouble that way. This leaves the rumormongers a clear field and an opportunity to fill the minds of people with false information. Once an individual has become convinced of something, even though it is based upon less than the truth, it is much harder to win that person over. A planning commission should seek to get to as many people as possible first and to convince them of the merits of its proposals.

Once this principle is accepted, the next question is what work of the commission should be put before the public. The answer to this, of course, is all of it—including information on what good planning is and can do. Forums and discussion meetings on the need for planning and the role it plays in government are a good means of gaining early support. In addition, press releases and discussions of the job of planning are important. The community should know just what the commission can and cannot do, and should not expect too much or accept too little. Once a planning program is under way, time and effort invested in community relations for the purpose of explaining the master plan and its purpose will pay big dividends. Zoning principles and purposes and the function of the zoning board of appeals are matters that can use plenty of explaining and public examination.

The more that is presented publicly in this fashion, the better informed both the members of the commission and the people at large will become. Naturally, any program of education or community relations will have to have behind it well-informed commission members,

The Citizen and Planning Action / 131

elected officials, and technicians. Each matter presented to the public must be supported by careful study, and the results must be presented in clear language. The manner in which the material is presented, whether in the press, radio, television, or public meeting, is also important. A good design or an attractive report can go a long way toward selling its contents. A poor presentation can sometimes lose support for an otherwise desirable proposal.

Throughout any program of community relations, it is important to be aware of the various publicity aids available. Primary among these is the press. An active, aggressive newspaper can be a valuable ally in furthering planning. Press releases should be prepared from time to time to aid the reporters and the editor in getting to the heart of what you are trying to do. The press should be encouraged to attend planning commission meetings, and its assistance should be actively sought. Radio and television are media that have a great influence on our public. I frequently feel that we are missing a golden opportunity to explain good planning by not having more programs on radio and television. In many cases, in the smaller communities particularly, stations welcome the chance to air programs with a local flavor. Public meetings and forums are also an excellent means of explaining planning. These need not be special meetings; local civic organizations can be asked to schedule a discussion of planning. The program chairperson of the Lions, Rotary, or Kiwanis Club is usually only too happy to know where a suitable topic and speaker can be found for a meeting. Other groups that should be kept informed include granges, fire companies, unions, women's clubs, and church organizations. They all can aid if informed, and at the same time many helpful suggestions and comments can be forthcoming.

In order to be able to tell its story, the commission should have some material for broad distribution. If an individual is able to take something away from a meeting, the possibility of his or her thinking further about it is increased. The material that is distributed should be carefully prepared and carefully chosen. This is not meant to imply that the public is entitled to know only certain things but that most citizens will not, in my experience, bother to read bulky documents. They are interested in facts, figures, and conclusions. They like to have their theory digested for them: the more concise the material, the more effective it is likely to be. Appropriate items for public distribution include:

1. Facts and figures, particularly those that show reasons for concern, needs, or conclusions. Population growth, land use in acres, school enrollment figures, and economic details are all of interest.

2. Findings and conclusions. These are the real heart of the matter and should be carefully stated. They can be effectively backed up by maps, charts, and graphs.

3. Summaries. Almost all of the work in planning can be summarized in a concise manner without losing its full significance. The preparation of a summary of a technical investigation will, in many cases, help the commission members themselves understand the work.

4. Maps. A self-explanatory map of a phase of the planning program can be very helpful. Care must be exercised, however, to make certain that no map is ever distributed that may be misleading or subject to easy misinterpretation. A good example of this would be a map showing proposed streets or roads before the alignments have been definitely and precisely established.

5. Ordinances. These are naturally a must for distribution. Often a simple explanatory statement attached to them can aid in offsetting emotional objections. It should always be made clear to the public that all ordinances will be subjected to a public hearing before being adopted.

It is equally important to recognize that certain things should not be distributed, either because they will not be effective or because they are certain to create trouble. The planning commission should not work in secret, and all of its study should be available to those interested in the full details, but those who are truly so interested are few. The material distributed should *not* include:

1. Technical tomes. Planning theory is all right in its place, but its place is not in the local barber shop or at neighborhood get-togethers. Formulas for appropriate amounts of commercial frontage per 100 of population or theories about the amount of traffic generation by two-story warehouses in the Mid-Atlantic states have little effect on hardheaded landowners.

2. Long, involved reports. A staff or consultant report may have to be long and detailed in order to examine all facets of a problem. This is for the commission's information and use, not to be broadly distributed. Don't expect the public to review any report of more than a few pages.

3. Material about which the commission members disagree. While a healthy divergence of opinion is a good thing, the commission should make certain that the basic principles presented in material that is distributed have been generally agreed to by the members.

4. A technician's report as a technician's report. This simply means that the quickest way to kill a planning study is for the planning board to sit back and receive a report, not to become a part of it, and to distribute it as the report of a professional. The technician is valuable only if used in an advisory role by the board. The material distributed must be accepted as the conclusions of the members of the duly appointed local body, arrived at with professional advice.

I MAY BE PERFECT BUT I STILL NEED ADVICE

Many communities find that their planning program can be greatly aided by the use of citizen advisory committees. Citizen committees are usually appointed by the mayor or the commission chairperson and should work directly with the commission. They can be helpful if properly organized and properly used. They can also be deadly harmful if created just for the sake of having a committee by that name, or if they are not properly handled. The question of whether or not a citizen advisory committee can be beneficial is a local problem to be evaluated by each community.

If it is decided to have such a committee, it should be remembered that as much care should be exercised in selecting its members as in the selection of the members of the planning board. Members should be interested citizens motivated by a genuine desire to help improve their community. While it would be impossible to organize any group of people who would all agree, it is not necessarily good to put the most vociferous objector to planning on the committee just for the sake of appeasement. Such a move has frequently backfired. All members of the committee should know that their responsibility is to work constructively with the commission, and all should be willing to do so. The members should also be selected to give the broadest possible representation from interest and geographic viewpoints.

An advisory committee can be used both as a sounding board for planning proposals and to perform certain tasks in conjunction with planning. The committee will be most effective when there is a definite program for its activity. Meetings should be well-organized, and the purpose of the committee clearly defined. Be as specific as possible and assign definite tasks to the committee. Never permit a citizens group to feel that it has been formed just to get a group of people together or simply because the commission wanted some one to rubber-stamp its action. Great care should be exercised to make certain that the committee does not wander aimlessly off on its own, and particularly that it does not become a mere front for political ambitions.

A word or two should be said here in the discussion of advisory groups about the upsweep in neighborhood activism. In both large and small cities, numbers of property owners bound together by a sense of commonality—whether by the threat of a new freeway or the intrusion of a large apartment complex into a single-family area—have organized neighborhood councils or people's action groups to protect their interest. While some of these quickly dissipate with the resolution of the crisis, many others become permanent, effective forces within the community structure. The latter are increasing, and future planning must take them into account. In point of fact, there are many who believe and say that, if planning is to be anything other than elitist control of resources, not only must it take into account neighborhood opinion and neighborhood organizations but it must start there as well.

It is obvious that, if we are to maintain a true sense of democratic action, we need to re-examine our governmental structure and devise ways for more meaningful citizen involvement and promote more responsive governmental agencies. One way of doing this would be through a carefully structured program for involvement of neighborhood councils in all decisionmaking. Although this may appear to be unwieldy, it may be necessary to avoid complete takeover of local government by Big Brother.

No planning program is going to be successful and no planning commission can say it is functioning properly unless there has been recognition of this grassroots movement. It must be shown also that careful attention is being paid to neighborhood planning and the desires and wishes of neighborhood residents. As noted in previous chapters, the format of the master plan is changing to that of a policies plan emphasizing goals and objectives concerning the kind of community the people living therein want to see. It is only logical that the rudimentary source for determining those goals and objectives lies in the neighborhoods and the structured organizations of those who feel a sense of common concern. The proper use of neighborhood planning techniques can well replace the need for a formalized citizens advisory committee, which frequently turns into a mirror image of the establishment or the power structure. At the very least, any formal organization of an advisory committee should be firmly founded on the principle of adequate representation and involvement from each identifiable neighborhood.

NOW LISTEN HERE, YOU BUREAUCRAT

This brings us to methods of formalizing citizen input through public meetings and required public hearings. Please note the purposeful differentiation. Public hearings are always required by statute, and many officials make the mistake of limiting citizen involvement to these alone. Public meetings are for discussion and the give-and-take of information. They can be held anywhere at any time but should never be held without adequate notice and publicity. Neighborhoods are an excellent locale for constructive and beneficial citizen meeting. Public hearings, on the other hand, are rather rigidly structured as to advertising, posting of notices, and the manner of reporting. Courts, when asked to review local action, are asking that a complete transcript of an official public hearing be taken. I feel that the conduct of both public meetings and public hearings is one of the most vital and important aspects of local government and of planning, and one to which too little attention has been paid. The manner in which these are conducted often determines the success or failure of a proposal or a plan. A tremendous responsibility thus rests upon the commission or agency, and in particular the chairperson, for the conduct of each meeting or hearing.

I have been present at dozens of these and have been amazed by the difference in them in various communities. One of the things that has bothered me most in the last few years is the deteriorating decorum of those who attend. Manners, courtesies, and just proper conduct seemingly are either being forgotten or else left at the door when people attend public hearings. I am sure that in many cases, if a movie were made, some of the individuals involved would find it hard to believe later that they were viewing themselves. I saw one hearing at which six rather large police officers lined the walls to maintain order—and it turned out to be fortunate that they were there. In many other hearings, invectives, profanity, and inhuman conduct have become commonplace.

Some of this results from the increasing frustration over nonresponsive government, and some comes from the observation of the effectiveness of civil disobedience movements and politics of conflict rather than compromise. While this is not the place to present a discourse on the general morals and code of conduct of the American people, it is important to note that in many cases such objectionable occurrences can be avoided by the manner in which the hearing or meeting is conducted. An efficient but firm chairperson who knows his or her business makes certain that the meeting never gets out of hand.

In zoning, both the zoning commission (which is in many cases the planning commission) and the governing body must conduct a public hearing before taking action. The zoning board of adjustment usually has to conduct a hearing before granting a variance. Newer zoning ordinances also require a hearing in conjunction with special exceptions, special use permits, or planned unit developments within the ordinance. The use of the planning commission as a review agency and the conductor of the hearing is becoming more common in the case of special provisions. In addition, the public hearing is required in connection with the adoption or change of the master plan and the approval of a major subdivision. As has been mentioned in an earlier chapter, in the case of urban renewal, several public hearings are necessary, including one by the planning commission concerning the declaration of blight. Capital improvement programs and budgets necessitate public hearings by both the planning commission and governing body before becoming official. This type of public involvement also may be required or scheduled even when not required for many other functions of local government.

In all cases, it should be remembered that the hearing has one purpose and one only. It is to permit the public to express its views officially in an orderly and constructive fashion. These views should be formulated in advance of the hearing by ample publicity and public meetings. Any material to be acted upon, together with supporting documents, should be readily available, published in the local paper, and generally explained in order to permit the public to be well-informed prior to the hearing. Maps and material needed for reference should be on display and easily accessible.

The meeting itself should be well organized. The chairperson, the key individual in the procedure, should present an opening statement setting forth the purpose of the meeting and the rules under which it will be conducted. It should be made absolutely clear that the hearing is neither a debate nor a political forum. Some additional suggestions that may be helpful in keeping your public hearing on track follow:

1. Before scheduling any public hearing, the responsible agency should have carefully studied the problems and should have its own house in order. No members of any commission, board, or agency should be permitted to sit in a public hearing until they can personally attest to the fact that they have studied the new zoning ordinance, reviewed the master plan, or are otherwise thoroughly aware of the case up for discussion.

2. The chairperson of the meeting should very carefully make a statement at the very beginning concerning the conduct of the meeting. He or she should let it be known just how the hearing will proceed and should make it clear that decorum and order will prevail. It should also be made clear that the agency conducting the meeting will not engage in lengthy discussions or debates with anyone. The purpose of holding the hearing is to listen to the views of the citizens of the community and then to evaluate the entire matter at a later date.

3. A secretary or stenographer should be present to take down careful notes, and, if possible, verbatim reporting should be provided. This not only ensures an accurate record but helps to keep the speechmaking to a minimum and the language above reproach.

4. The subject under consideration should have been made public sometime prior to the meeting, and there should be no necessity for any formal presentation during this meeting. Each person

should be instructed to give his or her full name and address and state his or her views as briefly and quickly as possible. Usually it is better to give all of those speaking *for* a particular proposal an opportunity to speak first to be followed by all of those opposed.

5. Upon the conclusion of each individual's statement, the chairperson should thank the speaker politely and assure the speaker that expressed views will be considered, and then move immediately on to the next person. No cross-examination or prolonged argumentative questioning of the commission members should be permitted.

6. Upon the conclusion of the statements of the public, the chairperson should again thank all for their interest and attendance and assure them that their views will be carefully studied and that the entire matter will be given full consideration by the body concerned. The meeting should then be adjourned. Careful study should be given to the record after it has been completely typed, for frequently the written word is subject to a different interpretation than the spoken.

7. The agency conducting the hearing should keep in mind the fact that there are many things that are necessary for consideration other than the expression of personal views. A public hearing should supplement the data-gathering, analysis, and discussions that have preceded the hearing, but at no time should the public hearing simply supplant this qualitative analysis. Above all else, the agency should remember that it is appointed or elected to represent not only the 50 or 60 people present at the hearing but also the other thousands of citizens of the community who did not attend or who did not express themselves publicly.

This last comment is an extremely important one. Time and again I have seen sound, desirable proposals killed by a wild and vocal group of 10 or 20 people. It is up to the hearing body to make certain that the opinions expressed, if they are in opposition to a proposal, are indicative of a general feeling within the community and not just the expression of a narrow and selfish interest. The public hearing can be a valuable means of ascertaining public opinion if it is properly conducted.

HOW CITIZEN INTEREST CAN BE EFFECTIVE

We have all heard that "you can't fight city hall." This has been (and is) true in many cases, but only because of the lack of an informed public, ineffective approaches, or disorganization. There is nothing more effective for quickly changing the mind of a public official, especially an elected one, than a sizable number of well-organized people who, through objective discussion and data collection, have gotten their act together. Having sat in the position of a city manager serving an elected commission both in front of the public and in private discussions, I have seen the results of such action. Unified, well-founded public opinion is still the most effective weapon in participatory democracy. The problem with most of us is that we don't want to bother with other people's opinions or with obtaining a concensus; we just want to see our own views reflected in every action taken. When we don't, we resort to that old American pastime of griping about "them" and what idiots and crooks "they" are. This all may be good for the blood pressure and personal satisfaction, but it leaves a lot to be desired in shaping community policy or winning the day for "our side."

This is not the way to be effective as a concerned person; indiscriminate griping has never solved many problems or gotten much accomplished. Citizen action need not be in a negative vein or in opposition to something proposed. Many times, positive things have taken place because of the foresight and determination of persons with no other concern than a genuine interest and caring. Parks have been built, open space preserved, libraries established, and planning agencies created because someone who cared would not take no for an answer.

On the western side of the City of Albuquerque, the land rises from the Rio Grande River to what is known as the West Mesa. In full view, as a scenic backdrop for the city along the western horizon, majestically protruding from the Mesa, are five extinct volcanoes. Around the volcanoes in the early '70s was nothing but sand, rocks, tumbleweeds, and rattlesnakes; but, as usual, developers began to think about the opportunities offered by the site. The volcanoes and the area in which they were located were not only scenic; there was considerable historic significance attached to them. Indian artifacts and signs of earlier cultures, rare organic materials, and some unusual vegetation abound in the area. No one had thought much about all of this until development became a possibility; then most seemed to accept the idea that rape by the developers was inevitable (after all, it had happened almost everywhere else in the area). Not so one marvelous, gentle, but determined woman, Ruth Eisenberg.

Coming to Albuquerque from Chicago in 1968, Ruth, being the kind of concerned individual she is, had immediately involved herself in learning about the city and trying to do what she could to make it better. Just to learn, she sat in on a class called "Creative City Watching" in the University of New Mexico's School of Architecture. Once, asking the professor what she could do to help put a stop to the rapidly vanishing attributes of the city, she was thrown this challenge: "Do something about the volcanoes." In all probability, that professor did not think what the ultimate result would be or even that he would hear again from Ruth about the issue.

To shorten the story unfairly, for there was a lot of frustration, dogged determination, research, arguments, and head knocking thrown in between, I recall with a great deal of pleasure the day when Ruth, with the equal persistence and help of the first woman ever elected to the city commission, could turn over the deed to the land (880 acres) upon which stood three of the five volcanoes. The story doesn't end there. Ruth, who kept on her almost single-handed fight, has now succeeded in snatching the other two out of the path of exploitive development and placed all of the remaining surrounding land (440 acres), including the other two volcanoes, in public ownership. There is still the opportunity for further enlargement into a major park and open space to be enjoyed by all, and there now exists a guaranteed protection of an irreplaceable scenic vista for the entire city.

Almost ironically some of the "establishment" that fought her the hardest joined hundreds of others in attending "An Evening at the Volancoes in Honor of Ruth Eisenberg," at which the mayor dedicated the new amphitheater at the base of one of the volcanoes to be named for her. Don't ever let anyone tell you that sincere interest and concern together with a determination to do something will not be effective. Ruth Eisenberg is living proof to the contrary.

The amazing thing is that most elected officials, as well as appointed commission members, welcome clear expression of formulated group opinion and agreement and will respond to it almost always. The obstacle is getting any group of two or more to reach that agreement or formulate a collective opinion, assuming it does not involve merely an issue that can be blown up into an emotional crisis. From my brief experience in politics, I have learned that the "pros" in the game quickly master the primary rules of all successful politicians: always postpone action on any controversial issue; don't take a position publicly until you see how the wind is blowing; and always look for, even encourage, dissension and disagreement among members of any delegation. An understanding of these gives a clue or two as to how to make citizen action more effective. In brief, a credo for doing so might run like this:

1. Make sure you have a real issue, not just a personal ax to grind.

2. Once you believe you have an issue, check it out to see how inclusive of others it is and make certain that it is a valid concern, not just something founded on rumors.

3. If there is no neighborhood council already in existence, get others together who should be interested and find out if they are informed and have some facts, not conjecture, to further inform them.

4. Assuming the issue is genuine and has held up through discussion and interest arousal, program carefully how you are going to get your act together.

5. Pick out any expertise in your group and get acceptance of responsibility for data collection, analysis, and presentation preparation. If possible, supplement this with aid from other citizen action groups, advocacy agencies, or a community design center (these exist in many cities).

6. Organize and plan your strategy, your timing, and your approach, making certain that you stay away from emotion and stick with facts. Avoid threats and implied intimidation.

7. As soon as you have enough data to begin to formulate a position, assign effective individuals to personal contact with key local officials and members of the "power structure," if they are known. No one in a position of influence or decision making likes to be surprised.

8. Get the troops out for the presentation, but be sure you have them well informed and under strict orders to stick with the "game plan" of your presentation. An effective maneuver is to have the opening speaker ask all of those interested in this issue and being represented to stand up. Keep them standing for a few minutes so that the "pros" can get a good idea of the head count.

9. Proceed with your informative and persuasive presentation, keeping it as concise and brief as possible. Have graphic materials and visual aids to help make points. Prepare something to leave with the hearing body, but keep it short and in summary form. Interestingly, one of the least effective things to leave is a petition. Too many of these have been shown to have been signed by those who will sign anything without knowing what it is about. There is no substitute for personal appearances for effectiveness.

10. Get a decision or get a definite timetable for action. Follow up and make certain that commitments are carried through. If and when favorable results occur don't forget to thank those who caused them to happen.

These are but some of the things to remember in making sure that the planning being done and other matters being dealt with on a day-to-day basis in your community is reflective of the true representative will of the people. The important thing is to overcome that old bromide of not being able to fight city hall and to recognize that people working together can and do make a difference. Just as in all matters of local government, this is essential for good planning. Even though planning done *for* us may help in correcting some mistakes from the past and in solving some problems, it is a much more satisfactory solution and comfortable feeling to know that what is being done under the aegis of planning is being done *by* and *with* us.

Planning for the future of our communities is vital to you and to me, and we are vital to good planning. I have tried to emphasize that point and to provide some touchstones toward a better understanding of the process. Each of us, the individual citizen, is the key to the future of our communities, whether they be large or small, urban or rural. If we keep interested and inquisitive, overcome discouragement and frustration, and are well informed and involved, we will have better places to live, work, and play—the kind of environment we all want and must have. If instead we leave our future to chance or the exploiters, we have no choice but to take the consequences; and we will have little justification for complaining about pollution, inconveniences, disorganization, or high taxes.

We must remember that our community, our society, will be, for better or for worse, what we make of it as individuals—by putting it all together collectively in our system of government. We have the responsibility to make it the best that we can, but to do so also makes good sense for each of us now and for those to come. No sector of organized society can long afford to be without the best possible planning for the best possible community of tomorrow. It just might be the most important issue facing us, not just for our comfort and convenience but for our very survival.

13. Some Things to Think About

In a concluding chapter, it seems wise to look back at some of the things
that have been said regarding the planning process of the past and
reflect on how it may be called upon to face current and future problems. No one is clairvoyant enough to look ahead with any degree of
accuracy. Were this not so we might have been able to avoid having to
try to cope with the automotive vehicle on streets designed for horse
and carriage. Who can say what strides will be made by technology in
the abatement of pollution within five years? On the other side of the
coin, however, there are those who say we have played out the string on
the ability of technical improvements to save us from ourselves and our
seemingly destructive tendencies. Whatever the case may be, the best
we can do at any given point is to anticipate and to plan based upon as
much information as we can gather, an intuitive analysis of the obvious
trends, and careful observation of the signs that can be read from our
social system. From then on, it is a matter of making the best value
judgments possible.

And the making of sound value judgments as a collective society, as
a government, particularly as it relates to the future, is where the going
gets tough. We seem to be imbued with a philosophy that as far as
government action is concerned it can and should be only reactive, not
preactive. We don't involve ourselves in prevention or protection, only
correction. We don't lessen the number of carbon-monoxide-produc-
ing engines on the streets until the accumulated pollution makes it so
unhealthy that it is necessary to declare a crisis; and then the solution is
only temporary. We don't take seriously the problem of inadequate
housing in the inner-city until we have had several incidents such as in

Newark or Watts. Thus, it seems that we are psychologically conditioned to crisis reaction instead of anticipatory positive change. This does not have to be the case: I still have hope that enough of us will be of this opinion to see that change will occur. Equally, I believe the process by which this can be accomplished is collective societal planning. It is also the greatest challenge and opportunity facing us today.

In the preceding chapters, we have seen how today's planning has evolved, how governmental activity in this area has grown, and how some of the earlier tools have been found to be in need of change although their principles have remained basic. We have reached the point at which federal policy seems destined to insist, if not demand, not only that there be local planning but also that this planning be an integral part of management. Whether we are willing to recognize it or not, history has shown us that when a function becomes an imperative by national policy or from a recognized national need, there is but a short time for local government to prove its capability to respond before the option of local response is threatened or removed. The crisis in urban life, both physical and social, is well accepted and has become one of those areas subject to national concern. How we respond at the neighborhood, community, city, and metropolitan level in showing our willingness and our ability to come to grips with our problems is going to have a great deal to do with the question of continuation of local self-determination.

It has been indicated that in community or individual decision-making we can make only the best possible value judgment in determining what action we take. Prior to that, however, we need to do some preparatory thinking about what we may have to face and the problems with which we may have to come to grips. For that reason, for what it may be worth, I will close out with the Smith synopsis of readings, from a rather cloudy crystal ball, of some of the major items that are becoming and/or will become issues and that will require planning involvement. This is not to say that this list will be all inclusive or that it is the sole responsibility of planners or planning to deal with them and magically produce solutions. It *is* to say that they are going to relate to issues that must be faced by decisionmakers and that planning can be a valuable tool in doing something about them effectively and intelligently. They fall generally into five categories—the inner-city, growth management, energy, delivery of services, and social concerns.

THE INNER-CITY

While things look a lot better for some cities in terms of the reversal of the outward movement of people and economy, all is still not rosy. Problems do and will remain, and, in all probability, some may even be aggravated if the so-called taxpayers revolt is widespread or long lasting. On the plus side, it can be seen that the energy situation and other factors have led to a rekindling of interest in older homes and apartment structures on the fringes of the inner core. Homes in the Capital Hill, Park Hills, and Curtis Park neighborhoods of Denver, all relatively near the central business district (CBD), were practically being given away some six years ago, but are now at a premium. A modest three-bedroom house, vintage 1935, will sell for anywhere from $75,000 to $95,000, depending upon location and condition. It is reported that real estate prices in Denver's inner-city have risen at a rate in excess of 12 percent per year over the last three years. This same situation holds true for other cities, as I have learned from talking to people in Portland, Baltimore, Atlanta, Minneapolis, and San Francisco.

With this resurgence and the advantages of revitalization and added ratables has come a new problem that is beginning to be of serious concern to sociologists, planners, and others. As always, when a new phenomenon occurs, we are quick to coin a new word for our planning and urban studies lexicon. The word of which we are going to hear more is "gentrification." In simple terms, this is used to describe the restoration of the "gentry" or well-to-do in what in most cases have been neighborhoods of the lower middle class and the poor. As interest in the closer-in areas is stimulated and as prices escalate, the low-income family is finding that, if they own their own home, (1) they cannot resist the prices being offered to them, (2) they cannot buy another in the same neighborhood (or probably anywhere at all), and (3) therefore they cannot afford to stick around and "keep up with the Joneses." Even more pronounced is the effect on those who are renters. Few absentee landlords are going to pause for even a brief moment to consider a lucrative offer for a property in which they have but a small investment and that has been a headache from the standpoint of demands for upkeep.

As these areas either house minority groups or were naturally integrated, the result is a return to segregation or stratification. As a consequence, we are now getting or will get in the future a new wave of the displaced poor. Gentrification, brought on by the economic forces at work in our capitalistic society and the recovery from the fear of the city, will bring about a number of new issues with which planning and planners must learn to contend.

Still, on the subject of housing, there are two other aspects which, while not new, must be apparent if we are to deal successfully with the inner-city. The first is the ever-present problem of adequate housing for low-income persons and families, which invariably means public or subsidized housing. With inflation, rising costs and interest rates, and a wave of conservatism appearing on the horizon, the difficulty of planning and carrying out suitable programs for this end of the economic spectrum will become even more frustrating and challenging. Large-scale, publicly financed, multi-unit projects will continue to be a must and hopefully will be dispersed throughout the urban area. To provide these in a way that makes sense and makes a contribution to society will require not only federal programs but also an intelligent, definitive housing policy—something of which we have long been in need but about which we continue only to skirt the edges and to which we only pay lip service.

There is evidence to indicate that the best answer to overcoming displacement and neighborhood destruction is to accelerate our programs for rehabilitation, conservation to keep those with pride where they are, and ways of maneuvering "the system" to get the moderately low-income people into existing structures. No better example of this can be found than the program being carried on by an organization known as Brothers Redevelopment, Inc., in the heart of urban Denver. Founded some six years ago by four committed individuals, all of whom are still involved in one way or another (Joe Giron and Manny Martinez on a full-time basis running the organization, Don Schierling serving as board of directors chairman while working as public affairs officer of the United Bank of Denver, and Dick Magnus—who is a Lutheran minister—as board secretary), BRI, as it is more familiarly known, operates as a nonprofit agency to save neighborhoods and to find ways of housing those who could not otherwise afford a decent place to live. Starting with a few gallons of donated paint and an offer to paint a home at no cost to the owner, they had trouble convincing their first "customer" they were for real and were not just going to "rip her off." Since then, they have renovated, remodeled, painted, fixed-up, and built over 450 units, all of which are a viable asset to the neighborhoods and the city. Their basic premise is that they are there to help those who need it and who are willing to help themselves. Using largely contributions of support money, materials, and equipment from private sources and some government funded jobs, many of which also provide on-the-job training to under-employed, their theory has been, "If you and your neighbors want to be part of the solution instead of part of the problem, let's pitch in and get to work. We supply the materials and supervision, and you supplement the labor." The amazing thing is how well it has worked.

Moving to the other end of the economic scale, those of us dependent upon the survival of the inner-city (and that includes all of us in my opinion) must realistically face the problem in the future of assuring a diversity of housing there. No central area can be considered to be sound economically on a long-term basis with only a nine-to-five daytime population. Even if low-income housing is dealt with by public funds, we will need to recognize the value of attracting private capital to invest in middle- and upper-income housing where it makes the most sense and is most efficient—in the downtown core. If this means tax abatement, special zoning, and even revenue bonds with favorable interest rates, then these are the things we must seriously study and consider. The mayor of Portland, Oregon, has created an organization called City Housing Development, Inc., with its board of directors comprised of himself and representatives of five major financial institutions. Their task has been to get large- and small-scale private residential projects into downtown Portland. They have successfully advocated or are considering, together with the city council, all of the above inducements and some others. A member of the city council in Denver has asked the Urban Observatory here to form a Task Force with some of us from the University of Colorado and the University of Denver to study this question and to recommend policy and program for the city to try to accomplish these same things. Every major city is or should be facing and anticipating the solution of this problem. The renewed desire to return to the city, the pressure of the energy shortage, and the recognition of the need to reduce pollution make the prospect of doing so an idea whose time has come.

Equally true is the value of good urban design in inner-city planning and, with that, thinking positively and imaginatively about downtown malls. Added to this should be a serious effort to find and use workable "people movers" in intensively developed areas, whether this be small electric buses, movable sidewalks, subways, or modes and means still in the idea stages. Regardless of the past condemnation of the downtown areas and the doom-and-gloom purveyors who continue to try to convince us all that anything resembling a central core is dead, within the last quarter of this century, with all the crises and shortages tumbling in on us, we are going to find that we cannot afford a "dead" center city. Unless a technological miracle occurs almost overnight, we are going to find that the day of the private automobile in the inner-city will have to be over. Some 25 years ago I remember making the statement in a speech at the University of Pennsylvania that there were those of us in the room who would see the day that the private automobile was at least restricted if not prohibited in the inner-city. In spite of general smiles of disbelief in that audience, I actually could say that I have already seen that "prophecy" fulfilled with the added limitations and restrictions in places like Philadelphia, New York, and Boston, but this is only the beginning of what is to come.

As we find the need to limit further individual automobile use, the feasibility and desirability of malls and the building-in of a sense of humanness in the downtown will be not only strengthened but a necessity and a way of life. Hopefully, good planning will find a way to convince investors that those steel and concrete monsters don't have to fill completely the land parcel at the ground level and that "people places" both enhance and ensure their investments. If you doubt this, just walk through the Skyline Park plazas in front of the Central Bank of Denver on a warm, sunshiny Colorado day or stand in the crowd at the plaza of Denver's First National Bank listening to a country-and-western band or a choral group perform and note the use people make of a little open space when given half a chance.

As to malls, the skeptics long have tried to convince us that they won't work, are a waste of money, and are a dismal failure, but they do work. The most cited example is that of Nicollet Mall in Minneapolis. This one development alone has shown that with sound planning, government, and private enterprise cooperation, and some ingenuity, a mall not only will work but it will be a foundation from which future downtown improvement can spring. In a publication entitled "American Urban Malls: A Compendium" prepared by the Institute for Environmental Action and the Center for Advanced Research in Urban and

Environmental Affairs of Columbia University, 68 functioning malls in American cities were reviewed and analyzed. Ranging in size from Toccoa, Georgia (population 8,000), to Philadelphia (1,950,089), facts are presented that show malls can and do work, if there are the same ingredients as in Minneapolis and there is a "planning attitude." How we handle people, aesthetics, and humanness in the inner-city is going to be of major concern in the future, and malls and people movers will have to play a vital role in our approach to solutions.

GROWTH MANAGEMENT

Whether we are considering a large or small urban area the problem of growth management will be another major issue. From those places that consciously seek to discourage additional expansion (and there are and will be those) to the ones concerned only with making certain that development is of good quality and properly directed, there will be a range of new techniques and methods tried to assure the desired results. The use of the planned unit development tool, whether in zoning or in separate legislation, will increase to the point of becoming commonplace. This will necessitate a close cooperation between policymaking bodies, planning departments, planning commissions, and developer-investors. Caution will need to be exerted to avoid decisions becoming so subjective that they are discriminatory, based only on individual discretion instead of founded upon easily understood and equitable standards. While additional flexibility is desirable in growth management and land development controls, the principle of "like circumstance-like treatment" will continue to prevail and deviations will be watched carefully by the courts. Good planned unit development ordinances can be found in almost all states now, and if you don't have one it is suggested that you contact your state planning agency or the American Planning Association, which can tell you where you can get a sample ordinance.

One of the newer tools in growth management, about which there has been a lot of discussion and about which there will be even more experimentation, is the transfer of development rights (TDR). Used in New York City as a means of encouraging the preservation of historic structures, the technique allows the establishment of a number of development units or rights that are assigned to landowners and are transferable from one parcel of property to another, thus becoming a marketable commodity. The March 1977 issue of *Practicing Planner,* a publication of the former American Institute of Planners, had a very good discussion of TDR, how it works, and the places it is now being tried as development form shaper in suburban and rural communities. These latter include Southhampton and Southeast in New York; St. George, Vermont; and South Brunswick, Hillsborough, and Chesterfield in New Jersey. As the article had as good an explanation of TDR as I have seen, portions are included here:

Transfer of development rights (TDR) attempts to preserve private property in the public interest without the expenditure of public funds for land acquisition. Put simply, TDR is a process by which the right to develop a parcel of land is separated from the parcel itself. Each remains private property and can be sold separately. The development rights can be sold to another party and used on a different parcel of land, thereby adding to the amount of development or density which can be built on the receiving parcel. ..."

TDR, while yet in the experimental stage, will be given a goodly amount of attention and assume an important role in land planning in the years to come.

Other techniques in growth management that should be noted and may be of assistance to local planning include "performance zoning" and "residential development review" ordinances. Both of these are methods of determining the impact of a development on an area or community, and approval is based upon a satisfactory finding of minimal impact and the meeting of established criteria. Performance zoning allows the developer a wide range of choices for development, permitting the mixing of single-family, multi-family, town houses, etc., in the same zone, but an overall density for the zone must be maintained. Bucks County, Pennsylvania, has been in the forefront with performance zoning and has published an excellent booklet on the subject. Marin County, California, uses the development review approach and in addition establishes an "annual residential growth quota" system to control the rate of growth.

ENERGY CONCERNS AND PLANNING

As we entered the last quarter of this century we found we can no longer take for granted the materials and techniques necessary to produce adequate energy for our way of life. In an earlier chapter, comments were made on the imbalance of consumption between our country and the rest of the world, particularly the developing nations. It is my belief that we are going to be faced with the necessity of severely adjusting our idea of a standard of living and that the conservation of energy utilization will be an important concern for tomorrow's planning. Just as in the discussion of malls, where it was suggested that the "freedom by choice" use of the automobile in the central city core that we have enjoyed may be approaching an end, we need to think much more seriously of alternative forms of transportation throughout the urban area. Immediately bicycles and mopeds occur as means of moving goods and people while conserving energy and reducing pollution. Unfortunately, in the past our planning effectuation to encourage and even allow this has been far from satisfactory. Instead of approaching two-wheeled vehicles as utilitarian modes of travel, we have persisted in the conception of them as being only recreational. Little has been done to make it safe and attractive to use a bicycle to go from home to work or to do the shopping. Planning for the 1980s is going to need to see that bikeways are raised in priority as a viable means of efficient transportation.

Other facets of energy-related problems about which planning will need to become more informed and active are the search for energy sources, the impaction of small towns from the extraction of these sources and energy development, and the new demands that will be placed on building codes from the development of solar energy and conservation measures in new structures. In the extraction of newly found oil, coal, uranium, and other energy sources, we will find an increasing dilemma facing rural areas and rural planners. Orderly land-use planning will be tested in trying to find ways to permit the mining, protect and encourage good development, and ensure the reclamation of the displaced land form. Several small cities in Wyoming, Colorado, and Montana have already been faced with the impaction predicament as they have become "boom towns" similar to those of the gold rush days. The mayors of Gillette, Wyoming, and Rangely, Colorado, for example, can give you an earful at any time about the trials and tribulations of having to prepare to become a big city with effective municipal services from a small economic base and tax base.

With regard to the effect of new energy forms and the need for conservation of available energy on local ordinances, several cities are moving in this direction by revising zoning ordinances to provide open-space requirements to protect solar installations from other structures, trees, and large bushes. Davis, California, appears to be one of the harbingers of things to come for a lot more of us with their energy conservation performance building code adopted in January 1976.

DELIVERY OF SERVICES

Should the California taxpayer revolt become a way of life, all levels of government will face an entirely new ball game on the question of delivery of services. Even if the drastic measures represented by California's "Proposition 13" are not emulated in other states, my crystal ball tells me that the money crunch in financing governmental services is real and is going to be around for some time. The cost of public education, as just one example, has risen from $2,653,000,000 in 1940 to $64,042,000,000 in 1971. Corresponding, but somewhat less drastic, increases have occurred in public welfare, police and fire protection, health care, refuse collection, and other services that we have come to take for granted. If revenue sources are limited and funds pegged in an inelastic position, the answer can lie only in one of two areas: either new sources of revenues must be found or services cut back. It is unlikely that taxpayers will permit these new sources simply to be other methods of taxing and even more unlikely that the federal government and states will relinquish the taxing base they have zealously protected over the years. This can leave the almost illegitimate children of our governmental structure, the municipalities, in the unenviable position of having to go to what has been referred to as "user charges." Carried to the extreme, this would mean that you and I would be charged a fee when our garbage is collected, the street is swept, or we call the police or need the fire department. These fees would have to be sizable enough to provide the basic financial support to keep the service in operation.

Whether this happens or not, we are coming into a new era of government financing that can and should mean an increasingly important role for careful planning. Every available dollar is going to have to be prioritized and used to produce the most good for the total community (a theory that is supposed to have been in effect for some time but that some of our governments seemed to have overlooked). The maintenance of existing capital investments in museums, libraries, streets, sewer systems, etc., will be a struggle in any budget planning, and new capital improvements programs will require even more justification as to the essential need for each project.

SOCIAL CONCERNS

It goes without saying after the previous section that social concerns and social programs are facing a running battle with the rising wave of fiscal conservatism. Therefore, the purpose here is not to belabor that point but to emphasize some happenings that will affect routine planning functions and are the result of changing social concepts. Most of these are coming from the enlarged social-arbiter role being played by the judicial branch of government. Court decisions have always set precedents for future action, but in recent years the opinions of judges in land-use and zoning cases have gone far beyond merely ruling on the legality of a particular question before them and have extended well into the field of social justice. Some of their written decisions have been well-worded lectures upbraiding recalcitrant municipal officials for failing to act in meeting a recognized social need or for appearing to want to retain an exclusionary or discriminatory environment through use of government regulation.

Comments have been made previously about the effect of the United States Supreme Court decision regarding school segregation and the enforced busing edict on school and neighborhood planning. This and similar landmark civil rights decisions of that court have set the stage for other federal courts and state courts to begin to apply the principles of equal opportunity for all more strongly in their consideration of planning and zoning cases. The most famous of these is that referred to as the *Mount Laurel* case (*Southern Burlington County NAACP* v. *Township of Mount Laurel*). Here the Supreme Court of New

Jersey, in a strongly worded opinion affirmed a lower-court decision that stated that one-acre zoning was an exclusionary measure and illegal. Justice Frederick Hall, a distinguished jurist then on the court, wrote the opinion, which said that every developing town must, through its zoning, make it possible for low-income families to find housing within its boundaries. The opinion further stated that the amount must be a "fair share" of the existing and projected need for this type of housing within the region in which the community is located. Many other things were said about not having as a prime purpose of zoning that of keeping taxes down or achieving a balanced budget, but the heart of the thrust of the comments was that each and every municipality must assume a responsibility for meeting the true require-ments for housing for lower-income levels in its socioeconomic region.

Most of the progressive-thinking zoning cases seem to come out of California and New Jersey courts, and shortly after the *Mount Laurel* case the matter again hit the New Jersey highest court in a different context. A developer had been given the "delay, linger and wait" treatment on a planned unit development that would have included a quantity of low-income units, and he finally took the matter to court. In *Oakwood at Madison* v. *Township of Madison,* the lower court, fol-lowing the dictum of *Mount Laurel,* chastized the Township, wrote a lengthy directing verdict, and even set numbers of types of units that the Township must permit. The Supreme Court upheld the decision in principle, reiterated the regional "fair share" concept, and said, "It is incumbent on the governing body to adjust its zoning regulations so as to render possible and feasible the least cost housing. . . . that private industry will undertake and in amounts sufficient to satisfy the deficit in the hypothesized fair share." The California Supreme Court picked up the "reasonably relates to the welfare of the region" in *Associated Home Builders of Greater East Bay, Inc* v. *City of Livermore.*

It seems clear that, while it may not have happened yet in your state, the courts are committed to regional concerns and the fair share concept in housing. This, in turn, will have a decided bearing on future planning and zoning. No longer will the rich, exclusive suburb be allowed to sit by complacently with a well-stocked treasury while the central city struggles to house and care for the urban poor. The courts and the Department of Housing and Urban Development (if the com-munity wants any federal funds) are going to insist that it can be shown that they are willing and able to do their "fair share." But just what is a fair share and how are regional needs to be determined? Regional Councils of Governments (COG's) exist in most states and have been the agencies that have been looked to to provide the information for this answer. As these are the agencies now being used for regional coordination review (A-95 Review) for all federally funded projects, and as the distributing center for some aid monies, they are in a position not only logically to provide regional information but also to be an effective force for some strong "moral persuasion" in the acceptance of the idea of sharing the housing and social load.

In Minnesota, the Metropolitan Council of the Twin Cities (St. Paul-Minneapolis) seems to be setting the example in many areas on how to find some solutions for regional problems. While it is an official regional council rather than a voluntary COG, the pattern being set is indicative of what can and should be done in every major metropolitan area if state legislators could put starch in their backbones and come to grips with the urban problems in their states. Here the council has taken the lead in establishing a regional housing need analysis and an allocation of a fair share on an individual municipal unit basis. The staff of the council prepared an allocation plan in 1971 and revised it in 1973 and again in 1976. As a result, the number of communities with subsidized housing has grown from 13 in 1971 to 90 in 1977. As Trudy McFall, director of the housing division of the council said in an article appearing in ASPO's *Planning* (August 1977), "That's a promising beginning." That also indicates the type of planning challenge that is ahead and will have to be met by other local and regional jurisdictions.

These are but a few of the important issues with which planning and planners are going to be called on to reckon. New ones will pop up all the time as we move into the wind-up of the 20th century and prepare for the next 100 years. As has been said probably far too often in this book, how we are prepared to cope with the problems of an increasingly complex and complicated society in a time of dwindling assets and resources is going to depend on our developing a collective "planning attitude" and on our established organized system of government (revised, modernized, or otherwise) seeing that we have plans that work. The alternative is, I am afraid, something to which none of us would want—or like—to look forward.

Glossary of Planning Terms

Included below is a brief discussion of some of the terms that anyone interested in planning may have heard or will hear in the future. No attempt has been made to include all of those about which some may have questions, even though the effort was made to be as explanatory as possible within the text. It is hoped that if there are those unanswered questions, they may lead the reader to contact persons involved with their own local planning and perhaps become better acquainted with the activity affecting them most directly.

AIP

The initials of the American Institute of Planners. Founded in 1917, this was the organization of professional planners in the United States until AIP consolidated with the American Society of Planning Officials in 1978. Membership required passing a test of planning competence after having gained experience through planning practice. AIP had standards for schools of planning that had to be met before an institution could be included in its list of recognized schools. When AIP and ASPO consolidated, the AIP certification processes became the responsibility of the American Institute of Certified Planners, a subsidiary of the new American Planning Association. AIP published the *AIP Journal, Practicing Planner,* and *AIP News.* Address: 1776 Massachusetts Avenue, Washington, D.C. 20036.

APA

An organization formed in 1978 through the consolidation of the American Institute of Planners and the American Society of Planning Officials. Members include professional planners, government officials, planning commissioners, and interested citizens. Its purpose is to encourage planning activity, provide information on the field of planning, conduct research, and serve as a clearing house for members and information. Membership is open to any interested individual. A subsidiary organization, the American Institute of Certified Planners, is open to professional planners who have passed certification tests. APA publications include *APA Journal, APA News, Land Use Law and Zoning Digest,* "Planning Advisory Service Reports," and *Planning* magazine. Address: 1313 East Sixtieth Street, Chicago, Illinois 60637, and 1776 Massachusetts Avenue, Washington, D.C. 20036.

ASPO

An organization of professional planners, government officials, planning commissioners, and interested citizens formally known as the American Society of Planning Officials. ASPO consolidated with the American Institute of Planners in 1978. ASPO's purpose was to encourage planning activity, provide educational materials, and serve as a clearing house for information or members. Membership was open to any interested individual. Publications included *Land Use Law and Zoning Digest, Planning* magazine, *TAB* (employment opportunities), and "Planning Advisory Service Reports." Address: 1313 East Sixtieth Street, Chicago, IL 60637.

CAG

Refers to citizen action group, which is a requirement for formalized citizen participation in the determination of where and how Community Development block grants will be spent. Since the inception of the requirement to show citizen involvement in community planning and action in the Federal Housing Act of 1954, the federal government has continued to increase its pressure for representative citizen involvement in policy determination in the use of aid money. Members of CAG's are usually appointed by the mayor, although in some instances election by districts may be used. In all cases, the membership is required to be representative of all geographic, economic, and ethnic groups.

CBD

Used in referring to the innermost core of an urban area—the central business district. There are no fixed standards for determining the physical demarkation of the CBD other than the area of the existence of the more intensified retail commercial and office concentration in the central core. While suburban and regional shopping centers have drained away the vitality of many CBD's, they remain that sector of the community with the greatest public investment in utilitiy installations and operational service costs.

CDBG

Community Development block grants. A term resulting from the passage of the Housing and Community Development Act of 1974 (Public Law 93-383). Under this legislation, the various community development programs administered by the Department of Housing and Urban Development were consolidated into a single block grant system. These included the formerly categorical (stated-purpose) funding programs for urban renewal, model cities, neighborhood facilities, open-space land, and basic water and sewer facilities. Within the guidelines adopted, local governments were given greater discretion as to where the money would be used. A principal purpose was to strengthen the ability of local government to "determine the community's development needs, set priorities, and allocate resources to various activities." State governments are eligible also. Grants are 100 percent funding without requiring a local match, although there are several stringent requirements that must be met for approval, including a housing assistance plan (HAP). This is aimed at requiring local government to "assess the housing needs of lower income persons residing in or expected to reside in the community."

CIP

Capital improvement program—the systematic organizing of the capital needs of a governmental unit into a plan for meeting those needs over a set period and within the financial capabilities of that unit. Considered to be a vital part of master planning, the CIP sets forth the essential facilities and service mechanisms necessary to support future growth and development as well as adequately service existing population. Included would be planning for streets, water and sewer facilities, parks, libraries, museums, police headquarters, city halls, and all other "capital" expenditures to be funded from public tax support or dedicated revenue funds. These expenditures are usually financed by bonds sold by the governmental unit and repaid over a fixed period from tax sources, primarily the real estate property tax. The CIP should be the basis for the capital improvements portion of each year's adopted municipal budget.

CLUSTER DEVELOPMENT (DENSITY CONTROL DEVELOPMENT)

A design technique permitted by many zoning ordinances that allows clustering of residential units on a smaller land parcel for each unit than specified as the minimum lot size for an individual unit. The controlling factor is that the normal average density for the zone must be maintained. If the zoning permits three units to the acre but requires a minimum lot 12,000 square feet, a developer's plan could be approved in which the units are "clustered" on individual parcels of only 6,000 square feet provided the density of three per acre is maintained. The remaining land is utilized for common open space or public use. The technique encourages innovative design and planning, saves development costs for the investor, and provides green areas and open space in common ownership for the residents. Some more sophisticated ordinances also use this same principle in planning for commercial and industrial development.

COG

Designates council of governments. These are voluntary organizations of local governments banding together to work on common regional problems. Membership in a COG is comprised of elected officials appointed by the governing bodies of the individual governmental units. There is usually an executive director and a professional staff. Originally started as an alternative to formalized metropolitan government and a means of cooperative regional planning in such matters as land use, transportation, air quality control, and delivery of services, COG's have become clearing house organizations for federally aided programs (in effect, almost subsidiary branches of some of the federal departments). Applications from local governments for federal grants are submitted through them for coordination clearing (A-95 Review) with proposed projects of other governmental units and with adopted master plans prior to being forwarded to the appropriate federal agency. In recent years, many COG's have become the transportation planning and coordination agency for their regions and administer Department of Transportation programs and funding as well as many of those of HUD and Health, Education, and Welfare. While COG's have no enforcement powers, their position in the allocation and distribution of federal aid has given them an influential role in many geographical areas.

EIS

Environmental impact statement. Created and popularized by the establishment of the Environmental Protection Agency (EPA), the EIS has now become one of the most potent tools in the planning process. An EIS consists of a detailed analysis of the impact of a proposed project upon the total environment—natural and man-made—within the general vicinity of the project or in an affected area at any distance. For example, through a challenge of the environmental impact, a multimillion-dollar dam project in the Tennessee Valley Authority area has now been stopped even though beyond 50 percent completion with the finding by the U.S. Supreme Court that an endangered species of marine life (the snail darter) would be destroyed by the impact of the completed project. Communities are discovering that an EIS on all major projects (not just those federally funded) is a useful means of making certain that good planning principles are followed and that areas beyond the project are adequately protected.

EMINENT DOMAIN

The power of government to acquire private property for public use for which the owner must receive "just compensation." This is an important tool of planning and is vital in capital improvements planning. An example might be that a master plan shows the alignment of a new collector street that would run through private property. The property can be acquired by the governmental unit by negotiation and purchase, or, if this fails, it can be "taken" through the use of "condemnation" under the right of eminent domain. Compensation is set by appraisals or, as a last resort, a condemnation court. Many special districts (authorities, school boards, water districts, etc.) and public utilities have been granted the "right" of eminent domain by the federal government and the states.

GENTRIFICATION

A word of recent vintage that portends an increasingly meaningful social dilemma. In simple terms, this refers to the trend of the return of the "gentry" or well-to-do to the inner-city residential areas, which is resulting in a displacement of lower-income persons, many of whom were renters. Older neighborhood homes are becoming more attractive to persons with means as the energy crisis continues and as city living once again becomes acceptable. The displacement of the poorer families creates a problem of finding adequate housing for them and begins the transfer of what probably has been a heterogeneous area back into a homogeneous one.

HUD

The Department of Housing and Urban Development established in 1965 as a cabinet-level department. All housing and many of the urban development programs were consolidated into the department. HUD is the agency administering the provisions of the various housing acts passed by Congress including urban renewal, federal aid for planning (Section 701 Program), open-space programs, neighborhood facilities, and basic water and sewer facilities. These have now been combined into special revenue sharing or block grant programs called Community Development block grants (CDBG) to be awarded to communities that qualify.

LPA

Local public agency—the way in which federal legislation refers to the governmental agency designated as the one responsible for administering the federal programs for urban renewal. LPA's could be the local governing body, a housing authority, or a separate urban renewal authority, depending upon the desires of the policymakers in the community. Due to the controversy and conflict in urban renewal, most municipal units chose to go the semi-autonomous urban renewal authority route. All funding for continuing or new renewal or rehabilitation projects now comes from Community Development block grant funding and must compete with other projects and programs for the available dollars.

MODEL CITIES PROGRAM

Part of the Demonstration Cities and Metropolitan Development Act passed in 1966, designed as a prototype program for the purpose of attacking physical, social, and economic ills in especially selected areas in approved cities. Federal money was used for housing rehabilitation, street and utility improvements, job opportunities, and welfare projects such as day-care centers, dental clinics, meals for the elderly, etc. The theory was that if you could put one neighborhood back on its feet, the cities would then extend such programs into other neighborhoods. A self-determining "Model Cities" neighborhood board was elected to participate in the allocation of the available funds. The program did not live up to expectations due to power struggles within neighborhoods, the devisiveness created between areas, and politics in general. Funds for the program were drastically reduced by the Nixon administration, and the categorical funding was eliminated by revenue sharing and the Community Development Act.

PERFORMANCE ZONING

A form of zoning developed to provide maximum flexibility in choice of use and design based upon an established density factor and measurement of impact of the finished product on the land and surrounding area. In a residential zone, a landowner or developer has the option of any type of residential unit construction, provided that standards of land-use-intensity measures, site variables, design variables, and facilities are met. Thus, a large tract of land has the potential of being developed as single-family, duplex, mobile home, patio house, town house, or apartments under the stated requirements pertaining to density, open space, and impervious surface created. This type of zoning has been most effectively used in Bucks County, Pennsylvania.

POLICE POWER

The power (or right) of government to restrict and regulate private rights pertaining to property and person for the public good. Such an action must be reasonable and in the interest of public health, safety, and/or general welfare. Examples of police power regulations are animal-control ordinances, building codes, traffic codes, zoning ordinances, and subdivision regulations. The use of the police power to restrict land use does not require that the owner of land be compensated.

PPBS

A method of budgeting referred to as planning, programming, budgeting system. As stated in "Management Policies in Local Government Finance," a publication of the International City Management Association, the PPBS "organizes goods and personnel into groups in order to carry out a defined purpose.... Specifically, the use of PPBS requires: (1) analyzing the objectives of city government spending and how well these objectives are being met; (2) carrying out detailed multiyear planning; and (3) setting up the necessary programming to present data in a form that can be used in making major decisions by the department heads, the city manager or other chief executive, and the finance officer. . . ."

PUD

The letters used to refer to planned unit development, one of the newer planning and zoning techniques. The original idea of PUD was to allow greater flexibility than could be achieved by traditional zoning in planning the development of large parcels of land. As an illustration, a 100-acre tract might have three or four fixed zoning areas (or even only one) and their rigid requirements (commercial only, apartments, single-family, etc.). The developer of the tract, by using the comprehensive master planning technique for the entire parcel, could request consideration of intermixed uses (apartments or offices over commercial, town houses mixed with apartments, compatible employment generators near residential, etc.) under standards adopted in a PUD ordinance or amendment and, if approved by the planning commission and the governing body, build over a period of time in accordance with the approved plan, which would be superimposed on and supersede the existing zoning requirements. The use of the PUD technique is a way to amend a zoning ordinance in accordance with a complete, coordinated plan of development for a larger parcel rather than piecemeal changes or variances of zone regulations. It should be remembered that the first step is the development and adoption of a carefully conceived PUD amendment to the zoning ordinance.

701 PROGRAM

A program started by Section 701 of the Federal Housing Act of 1954. This was the entry of the federal government into financial grants for comprehensive planning purposes. Through state agencies, funds were made available to municipalities to pay for planning studies and plan development, first on a 50-50 basis and later on a 75-25 match. This was the "carrot" portion of the "carrot and big stick" approach of the 1954 act that greatly increased local planning activity and master plan preparation.

TDR

Transfer of development rights—a system of land development control wherein rights or development units are assigned to each parcel of land based upon planning studies and density control factors. These rights are separable and may be transferred to other parcels; thus, they are marketable. A piece of land may be unsuitable for intensive development due to any number of factors yet lie in a zone where such development is allowable. By the use of TDR, the owner of the property can be compensated from private sources for the usable rights, which are then transferred to other land more suitable for intensive development. Once development rights are transferred, the decreased utilization right becomes a restriction on the future use of the originating property and runs with the land.

WPCI

Workable program for community improvement—a provision of the 1954 Federal Housing Act that initiated the requirement of measurement criteria for determining community action for improvement for any local government seeking federal funds for urban renewal. Seven items of evaluation were included. The first and most fundamental one was that there be a comprehensive master plan for total future development. This "big stick" approach resulted in a great increase in the number of local planning commissions and master plans. The WPCI also began the federal insistence on citizen involvement in planning and urban renewal activity.

Appendix A

COMPREHENSIVE PLAN DRAFT:
DENVER, COLORADO (EXCERPT)

COMPREHENSIVE PLAN DRAFT

PRELIMINARY GOALS

AS PREVIOUSLY PRESENTED IN <u>PRELIMINARY COMPREHENSIVE PLANNING GOALS AND OBJECTIVES FOR DENVER</u>

VIABILITY

To foster a city of quality that sustains itself through effective and mutually supportive physical, economic, and social systems; that rewards its citizens by fulfilling their common aspirations while maximizing individual growth potential and freedom of choice; and that successfully competes for an equitable share of the region's future growth.

STABILITY

To identify and protect the physical, economic, and social assets of the City's past and present development as a basis on which to build the future.

ADAPTABILITY

To be responsive to potentially constructive changes in the physical, economic, and social conditions of the City.

DIVERSITY

To provide a variety of community activities and services, and to provide a wide range of choice in life styles.

OPPORTUNITY

To provide every member of the community with the chance to participate equitably in the life, rewards, and responsibilities of the community.

AMENITY

To support community activities with a desirable, convenient, attractive, comfortable, and enjoyable environment.

Neighborhood plans will become the development guides for the areas for which they are prepared, within the context of the broader citywide plan. Policies contained in the citywide portion of the comprehensive plan were prepared with careful attention to the needs of residential neighborhoods. Therefore, it is expected that neighborhood plans will be prepared within the framework of citywide plan policies, and thus be compatible with and supportive of the citywide plan. It is recognized, however, that adopted neighborhood plans may alter or supplement citywide policies for local application. They will serve as the development guides for the neighborhoods for which they are prepared. As such, they will guide both public and private development and redevelopment decisions, and will guide the planning office recommendations to the mayor and city council on matters such as zone change requests, street construction and vacations, and the placement of public facilities.

Neighborhood plans allow for flexibility in recognition of diversity among neighborhoods. Plans include a plan map that is more specific and detailed as to planned land uses, public facilities and transportation routes than the citywide plan maps. They address land use, housing, transportation and public facilities primarily, but may address other issues and concerns that are not addressed in the citywide plan and are unique to the specific neighborhood. In this way, there are opportunities for greater flexibility in the neighborhood plans and planning process in recognition of neighborhood diversity.

Neighborhood plans make recommendations for improving neighborhoods. They make recommendations that may be implemented immediately or over time for land use, transportation, housing, public facilities and environmental improvements to the neighborhood. They may also include recommendations about neighborhood organizations, improvement of city services, needed social services, and private development. It is expected that these recommendations will become a guide for public action and private investment, as well as one program of action for the neighborhood organization.

The Neighborhood Planning Guide, issued by the Denver Planning Office in October, 1976, describes the joint neighborhood-city effort that goes into the preparation of a neighborhood plan. Neighborhoods are selected from a citywide analysis of socio-economic conditions, other objective factors, and the expressed interest of residents. The final selection results from an information presentation of a neighborhood analysis to the Denver Planning Board and to a meeting of neighborhood residents, businessmen, property owners, institutional and social agency representatives, and any other groups with an interest in the neighborhood. The neighborhood planning team of 10 to 20 members is then selected by election, volunteers, or appointment by the neighborhood planner, the neighborhood organization or some combination, depending on the degree of interest exhibited by the citizens. Every effort is made to notify and involve all segments of the neighborhood, especially residents, in the preparation of a neighborhood plan.

Neighborhood organizations may prepare neighborhood plans with assistance from the planning office. When this occurs – and prior to starting the preparation of a neighborhood plan – the sponsoring group or organization will be requested to consult with the planning office. In this manner, the neighborhood planning staff can provide needed maps, demographic data and other information, aid in insuring that the group is representative, and serve as resource persons or observers during the course of plan preparation. In addition, planning office staff will assist in conducting the same type of review process that all neighborhood plans undergo for adoption: neighborhood public hearings, city agencies, the planning board, mayor and city council.

Neighborhood plans primarily address issues of concern to one neighborhood. Whether the plan is prepared under the city's existing neighborhood planning procedure or by a group within the neighborhood, for those issues that affect broader concerns (more than one neighborhood or the entire city), all concerned interests will be brought together in the planning process.

OTHER SMALL AREA PLANS

The Denver Planning Office also prepares plans for small areas such as Downtown Denver, the Platte River Valley, and activity centers. These plans are prepared in close consultation with the affected interest groups and concerned citizens in much the same way as neighborhood plans are prepared. They also can supplement or amend the comprehensive plan.

POLICY PLANNING APPROACH

BACKGROUND

An important characteristic of the citywide plan is that it is policy-oriented. Since it is central to the plan, it is useful to explain the elements of policy planning. Policy planning identifies idealistic and abstract goals and refines them successively into more realistic and explicit objectives, policies and programs.

Commonly held goals and objectives are important to policy planning. They serve several purposes. First, they permit the coordination of efforts to improve the condition of the city. Coordination is necessary because countless public and private decisions affecting the city's future are made daily. Although these decisions represent specific needs and desires, it is important that their combined affect on the general well-being of the city be positive. Second, goals and objectives provide the basis for selecting appropriate policies and programs for community improvements and for evaluating their relative success during and after implementation.

Goals are very general long-term aims or desired ends toward which resources to improve the condition of the city should be directed. The goals for Denver are presented at the end of this section.

Long-Term Objectives are derived from goals and are somewhat more specific statements of general aims related to one of the four major sections of the citywide plan - land use, transportation, public facilities, and the environment. Long-term objectives are placed at the beginning of each section to provide a frame of reference for the section's policies.

Policies more specifically define long-term objectives. They identify general courses of action for implementing long-term objectives. Policies in the citywide plan are further grouped into more specific subjects. For example, policies are presented separately for residential areas, housing, business areas and industrial areas within the land use section.

Short-Term Objectives are desired ends proposed to achieve specific aspects of policies in relatively short periods of time. They are realistic, and are capable of being measured and evaluated as to the extent of their accomplishment.

The first set of short-term objectives will be prepared as part of the continuing planning process after adoption of the plan. The types of short-term objectives will vary. For instance, they may call for the provision of information, the preparation of technical studies, assistance to citizen and other groups, the establishment of specific programs, or the construction of specific public improvements.

Progress toward achieving short-term objectives will be assessed annually or biennially as part of the continuing planning process. Progress will be measured primarily through analysis of selected statistics. Statistical information to aid in this review is presently available for housing and population, building activity and demolitions, land use, and household characteristics. In addition, special surveys will be conducted as needed.

Once prepared, short-term objectives will be periodically evaluated and modified as necessary. Objectives that have been achieved will be removed and those that require further effort will be retained or modified as necessary. New objectives will be established as needs are identified and as resources to meet those needs become evident.

Programs are outlines of specific activities to be performed in achieving goals and objectives and in implementing policies. Some programs are already established. Others are proposed by the citywide plan or neighborhood plans. Still others will have to be developed as part of the continuing planning process.

GOALS FOR DENVER

● Viability - To foster a city of quality that sustains itself through effective and mutually supportive physical, economic and social systems; and that rewards its citizens by fulfilling their common aspirations while maximizing individual growth potential and freedom of choice.

● Stability - To maintain the present physical, economic and social assets of the city as a basis on which to build the future.

● Adaptability - To be responsive to potentially constructive changes in the physical, economic and social conditions of the city.

● Diversity - To provide for a variety of community activities and services, and to provide for a wide range of choice in life styles.

● Opportunity - To provide every member of the community with the chance to participate equitably in the life, rewards and responsibilities of the community.

● Amenity - To support community activities with a desirable, convenient, attractive, comfortable, healthful and enjoyable environment.

CITYWIDE PLAN
====================

PLANNING FOR LAND USE

LONG-TERM OBJECTIVES

● To preserve physically sound residential, shopping and employment areas, and to protect them from intrusion by incompatible land uses and activities.

● To rehabilitate and/or redevelop physically unsound residential, shopping and employment areas.

● To maintain and develop distinctive characteristics of physically sound residential, shopping and employment areas.

● To effectively use undeveloped and underdeveloped land.

● To guide new development, redevelopment and rehabilitation in a manner that will reflect identity, harmony, variety and quality in design.

● To achieve a reasonable balance between different land uses and activities.

● To provide sufficient land suitably located and serviced to accommodate a desirable mix of residential, shopping and employment activities.

● To conserve the city's existing supply of sound housing, and to prevent deterioration of its condition.

● To provide for a variety of housing types and styles for various income levels and family types.

PLANNING FOR LAND USE: GENERAL

BACKGROUND

This section of the citywide plan provides an overall guide to general land use development of the city. It sets forth policies to guide the changing pattern, intensity and timing of development for residential, commercial and industrial uses. The general pattern and intensity for each type of land use is also portrayed graphically within the respective sections of the plan.

Denver's general land use pattern consists of three distinct concentrations:

● Industrial land uses are predominantly concentrated in the South Platte River Valley and along Interstate 70 leading east to Stapleton International Airport and beyond.

● Commercial land uses are concentrated in Downtown Denver and extend outward in linear fashion along major transportation routes.

● Residential land uses are developed in a concentric pattern around the central part of the city, with multi-family structures predominantly concentrated adjacent to downtown, and single-family houses becoming the predominant pattern outward from the downtown area.

POLICIES

General business policies apply to more than one type of business area and attempt to properly relate business uses with other elements of the citywide and neighborhood plans.

B1. DEVELOPMENT OF LAND ALREADY ZONED FOR COMMERCIAL USES SHOULD BE
     ENCOURAGED PRIOR TO REZONING OF ADDITIONAL LAND

     Land use in the city is not static, but there should be valid reasons for changing the existing uses. Requests for additional commercial zoning should be carefully analyzed to verify whether or not conditions have changed sufficiently to warrant approval of the request. Before business uses are allowed to expand or intensify, a clear need should be demonstrated and protection of adjacent uses assured. However, care should be taken that the normal supply and demand of commercial-zoned land is not altered in such a way that adverse economic impacts are created for the community in general.

B2. EXPANSION OF BUSINESS USES INTO OR WITHIN RESIDENTIAL AREAS SHOULD BE
     PERMITTED ONLY IF SUCH EXPANSION MAINTAINS OR IMPROVES THE RESIDENTIAL
     DESIRABILITY OF THE AFFECTED NEIGHBORHOODS

     If such expansion occurs, efforts should be made to improve the relationship between the businesses and the neighborhood. Proper vehicular access should be provided, and consideration should be given to the design, location and arrangement of buildings, parking areas, signs and lights. Effective vegetation or architectural buffers should be provided between business and residential uses.

B3. THE CITY SHOULD ENCOURAGE ALL BUSINESS AREAS TO DEVELOP AND MAINTAIN A
     PLEASING ENVIRONMENT

     A pleasing shopping environment is desirable for people who use the area, to attract new shoppers, and for nearby residents to enjoy. New structures should be designed with an awareness of the impact that they will have on the larger visual environment of the area. Efforts should be extended beyond the minimal needs of public health and safety. Older areas require better structural and site maintenance. Consideration should be given to proper landscaping; screening of lights, fumes, and noise from adjoining areas; control of internal auto-pedestrian circulation; access; protection of pedestrians; and provision of open space. Outdoor lighting and advertising signs should be designed to enhance the visual qualities of Denver.

B4. MAJOR BUSINESS AREA CONCENTRATIONS, ESPECIALLY NEW DEVELOPMENT, SHOULD BE
     ENCOURAGED TO UTILIZE MULTIPLE ENERGY SOURCES

     With continuing concerns about the adequacy of future energy supplies, the conservation of current supplies should be supported by the use of alternative energy sources, such as solar energy. In addition to technical and regulatory (building codes) measures, energy considerations should be included in the process of determining the type, location and intensity of development.

The Downtown Denver area is the center of both the region's and city's business activity. The intensity of activity offers advantages not provided elsewhere in the region. In addition to some high-density residential development, it contains the metropolitan area's primary concentrations of government, finance, cultural

PLANNING FOR LAND USE: BUSINESS AREAS

BACKGROUND

Historically, business development in Denver began in the area known as 'lower downtown.' From there it expanded to the present downtown area and as strip commercial along developing trolley lines. With housing constructed adjacent to the strip commercial, an inevitable conflict occurred as businesses prospered and required room for expansion. When the auto replaced the trolley, another type of conflict arose: traffic seeking through movement on arterial streets came into conflict with traffic desiring to enter and leave local businesses. Problems of land use and traffic conflict both remain with us today.

Decentralization of businesses began when groups of businesses began locating near centers of outlying population concentrations. This generally occurred within residential neighborhoods at intersections of relatively busy streets. During the 1950's, the trend continued in Denver with the emergence of shopping centers, typically serving larger trade areas. These centers contained larger groupings of businesses and ample off-street parking.

A wide variety of activities ranging from retail and wholesale trade to general business and professional and personal services are now located in Denver's business areas. In 1975, about 50% of Denver's labor force, or an estimated 159,000 people, were employed in these activities. Yet these activities take place on the smallest amount of land used for any purpose in the city. Business areas attract more people per acre for continuous use than any other type of land use. Location, siting and accessibility affect not only the immediate development, but also the surrounding areas. Constant efforts must be made to find ways of minimizing conflicts between business and other land uses.

The amount of land zoned for commercial development in Denver is more than adequate. Nearly one-fourth of the city's commercially zoned land is vacant and approximately one-third contains uses other than commercial. A related problem is that over one and one-half square miles of land zoned for other purposes are used for business activities.

Many of Denver's business areas are stable, but a number have declined in recent years because of suburbanization; inadequate auto access and parking; obsolete facilities; unattractive shopping environments; and changes in the shopping habits, income and number of trade area customers. Some of these areas still have strong market potential and if renewed or rehabilitated could compete effectively. Others may have outlived their usefulness.

Well located and competitive business areas that are accessible, attractive and convenient, must be maintained within the city if Denver's citizens are to be provided with needed commercial services and jobs. An economic development strategy for Denver must recognize that one of Denver's prime economic resources is its people and their potential. Such a strategy must offer incentives to maintain, improve and expand existing businesses while encouraging new business to locate in the city. The city should also develop policies that will improve its environment to retain present residents and attract new residents. These efforts would also help to increase the demand for retail goods and services, and create jobs for present residents, especially unemployed and underemployed low-income people.

facilities, entertainment and general business activities with nearby access to education and sports facilities. The <u>downtown adjacent areas</u> contain many of the same commercial functions as the downtown, but at a lesser intensity. They also contain general industrial, wholesale, related services uses, and high-density residential development. Because of the generally mixed character and considerably lower intensity of development, these areas are supportive of, rather than competitive with, the downtown area.

B5.   DENVER'S DOWNTOWN DEVELOPMENT SHOULD BUILD ON THE ACTIVITY AND STRENGTH OF ITS COMMERCIAL CORE AREA

This area, generally bounded by 14th, Larimer and 18th Streets, and Lincoln and Colfax Avenues, is the heart of downtown for most people. Within this central high-density district are located the regional centers for shopping, finance and employment. Future development of this core area should contribute to its compactness, density and 'walkability.' The major office, apartment and hotel buildings added to the core area in the past ten years indicate the strong trend toward higher intensity. This trend is favorable, provided that new building design reinforces a unified pattern of street activity and adds to pedestrian interest by encouraging the formation of usable open space and a variety of ground level shops, and that transit service keeps pace with the higher numbers of people using this area daily. The proposed pedestrian transit mall would provide the major unifying element for the downtown while serving as the linear link between the many downtown area activities. Recognizing that the provision of mass transit alone cannot decrease auto dependence, disincentives to auto commutation into the downtown area as well as within Denver and the metropolitan area should be explored for implementation.

B6.   THE LAND USE AND DENSITY OF THE DOWNTOWN CORE AREA SHOULD CONTINUE TO CON-TRIBUTE TO A DISTRICT OF INTENSIVE BUSINESS ACTIVITY, WITH APPROPRIATE ACCOMPANYING RESIDENTIAL USES

Keeping the downtown core area a compact, high-density commercial district with appropriate accompanying residential uses benefits downtown businesses, their employees, visitors, shoppers and residents of the area. The compact core provides for easy pedestrian movement between businesses and keeps the various districts economically supportive of each other while high employment density provides better support for increased transit usage. For residents, the high-density commercial usages, if accompanied by retail facilities for daily necessities, provide a way of life that is itself compact and stimulating. For pedestrians, greater visual interest is created with fewer distractions or conflicts if continuous building frontage is not interrupted by driveways and constant encounters with vehicles. Parking facilities should be mostly located on the perimeter to emphasize pedestrian movement in the high-density linear core. Efforts should be made to encourage downtown parking facility use for short-term shopper and visitor parking rather than long-term commuter parking.

B7.   THE TRANSPORTATION SYSTEM SHOULD PROVIDE PEOPLE WITH GOOD ACCESS TO DOWN-TOWN LOCATIONS, BUT NOT UNLIMITED MOVEMENT OF VEHICLES WITHIN THE DOWNTOWN AREA

Downtown access should be provided by several means: express bus service to downtown transfer points at both ends of the core area coupled with internal transit shuttle to final destination; regular local bus service

primarily along major streets with most routes having stops at downtown
transfer points; auto movement from arterials at the periphery of downtown to long-term parking facilities at the edge of the core, or short-
term smaller parking facilities within the core area; and bicycle routes
to and within the core area. Additionally, efforts to explore the feasibility of rapid transit should continue.

B8. DOWNTOWN AND ADJACENT NEIGHBORHOODS SHOULD BE MUTUALLY SUPPORTIVE OF
EACH OTHER

Some adjacent areas have the potential for additional housing development,
with related commercial activity, as does downtown itself. Downtown planning and development should support recent trends toward the preservation
of nearby neighborhoods and special historic districts, the reuse of older
structures for residential development, and the increasing interest for
living in and near downtown.

B9. AN INTEGRATED AND MIXED-USE REDEVELOPMENT OF THE CENTRAL PLATTE VALLEY,
WHICH WOULD BENEFIT THE CENTRAL AREA OF THE CITY SOCIALLY, ECONOMICALLY
AND ENVIRONMENTALLY, SHOULD REPLACE THE PRESENT RAILROAD YARDS

The redevelopment of the Central Platte Valley - generally bounded by I-25,
West Colfax Avenue, Auraria Higher Education Center, Union Station, and
23rd Street - for residential, commercial, recreational, and/or industrial
uses should be encouraged. It is recognized that no commitments have been
made to redevelop the area, and that the area may continue in its present
use in the near future. Should redevelopment occur, however, it should be
consistent with the policies stated in the Denver Planning Board Resolution
of March 2, 1977. These policies provide the guidelines for residential
densities; park and recreational land and opportunities in conjunction with
the Platte River greenway; accessibility to surrounding areas; flood plain
ordinance compatibility; commercial, industrial, community facilities and
transportation development; environmental concerns; and the fiscal impacts
of the proposed development.

Mixed residential/commercial areas consist of groupings of establishments that
normally provide similar or supportive services (such as office complexes, entertainment districts and private medical centers) along with high-density residential development. These groupings offer advantages for both the establishments
and the public they serve.

B10. SOME OFFICES AND SIMILAR FACILITIES SHOULD BE CLUSTERED WITH RESIDENTIAL
USES AND LOCATED OUTSIDE OF THE DOWNTOWN AREA

Current trends indicate that Denver, because of its central location in
the region, will continue to attract new office development. Some types
of offices can function outside of the downtown area and in combination
with residential uses. Locations selected for these mixed uses should
minimize negative impacts on all supporting systems and surrounding areas.
Transportation access is also important in selecting locations. When
these mixed uses are located adjacent to existing or planned retail
areas, mutually reinforcing opportunities offer advantages not found
in isolated locations.

MASTER PLAN POLICIES SECTION:
ALBUQUERQUE, NEW MEXICO (EXCERPT)

2. Urban Areas

THE GOAL IS A QUALITY URBAN ENVIRONMENT WHICH PERPETUATES THE TRADITION OF IDENTIFIABLE, INDIVIDUALISTIC COMMUNITIES WITHIN THE METROPOLITAN AREA AND OFFERS VARIETY AND MAXIMUM CHOICE IN HOUSING, WORK AREAS AND LIFE STYLES,[1] WHILE CREATING VISUALLY PLEASING ARCHITECTURE, LANDSCAPING AND VISTAS TO ENHANCE THE APPEARANCE OF THE COMMUNITY.

POLICIES

PROPOSED TECHNIQUES

a. Redevelopment and rehabilitation of older neighborhoods should be continued and expanded.x

1) Designate Neighborhood Development Plan (NDP) areas for each neighborhood in the City with a strong emphasis on citizen participation.

2) Design Neighborhood Development Plans for particular areas of the City, containing a specific set of development guidelines, capable of dealing with unique development patterns and concerns.

3) Provide rehabilitation funds for both residential and commercial uses and methods for financing which owners can · afford (e.g. improvement districts, incremental financing, U.S. Federal Community Development Block Grant funds, General Revenue Sharing funds, "homesteading").

4) Initiate combined residential/commercial zones.

5) Provide incentive for rehabilitation by upgrading and maintenance of public improvements.

6) Provide for demolition and clearance (where appropriate) and redevelopment of vacant land.

7) Review all neighborhoods and update NDP on a regular basis, analyze trends, identify new opportunities and develop solutions to cope with changes in the neighborhood.

b. Selected buildings and areas which explain our past and which give Albuquerque identity, individuality and cultural richness shall be preserved, enhanced and reused where appropriate.

1) Continue and support inventory of historical and cultural properties of significant local interest.

2) Develop detailed area plans specifying buildings and areas of preservation.

3) Acquire historical and cultural properties of significant local interest through public or private efforts where necessary to prevent demolition or other loss.

4) Support creation of a broadly-based non-profit organization which could sponsor and initiate preservation efforts.

5) Investigate new techniques for preservation such as "homesteading" and tax incentives.

Appendix B

CAPITAL IMPROVMENTS PROGRAM:
ALBUQUERQUE (EXCERPT)

CAPITAL IMPROVEMENTS PROGRAM
May 1974 Election

This document contains the list of projects which will be put to the voters, by purpose, for approval during May 1974. This program, which basically incudes projects to be constructed for fiscal years 1975 and 1976, has undergone careful review by the operating departments involded, the Planning Department, the Capital Improvements Committee, the Environmental Planning Commission, and the City Commission.

Basically, the program features the following:

- This Capital Improvements Program, if given voter approval, will allow property taxes to remain at the existing level. Under this provision, a program of $20 million of general obligation bonds can be financed.

- The projects funded by general obligation bonds in this program are to serve existing development within the city limits and are to encourage infill development. In fact, 19 out of every 20 dollars of public works projects are to serve the current residents. The general obligation bond program, therefore, allows for very little growth outside the city limits.

- The $20 million bond request will allow for federal and state matching funds as well as expenditures from other sources to bring the total capital expenditure to about $60 million.

Since the General Obligation Bond funds which the voters are asked to approve contain little provision for new growth and development, it is proposed that future growth in new areas be funded by a new source of revenue. Should that new source be found, the capital program calls for the following additions to be made:

- Any new source of revenue would be used to finance water and liquid waste extension.

- Approximately $11 million of new city revenues would be required to allow the needed expansion. This amount would provide for an additional 12,000 persons per year for the next four years.

In the pages that follow are detailed lists of projects, maps, and financial information on the General Obligation package to be put up for voter approval this May. In addition, a separate listing of those projects which would be constructed in the event new revenue is obtained, can be found under the water and liquid waste listings.

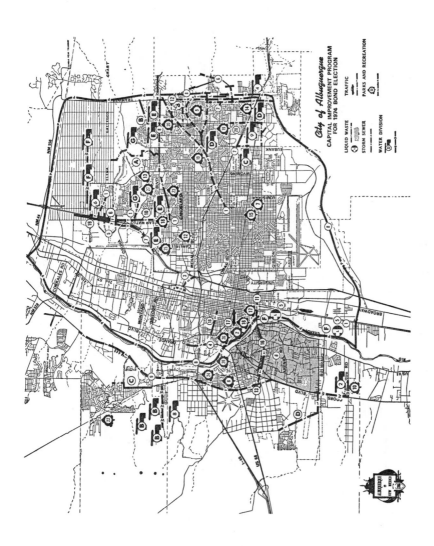

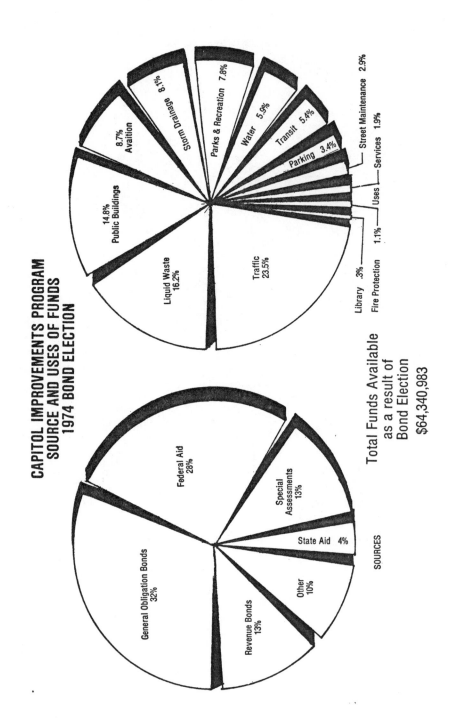

CAPITOL IMPROVEMENTS PROGRAM
SOURCE AND USES OF FUNDS
1974 BOND ELECTION

USES

Traffic 23.5%
Liquid Waste 16.2%
Public Buildings 14.8%
Avaition 8.7%
Storm Drainage 8.1%
Parks & Recreation 7.8%
Water 5.9%
Transit 5.4%
Parking 3.4%
Street Maintenance 2.9%
Services 1.9%
Fire Protection 1.1%
Library .3%

SOURCES

General Obligation Bonds 32%
Federal Aid 28%
Special Assessments 13%
Revenue Bonds 13%
Other 10%
State Aid 4%

Total Funds Available
as a result of
Bond Election
$64,340,983

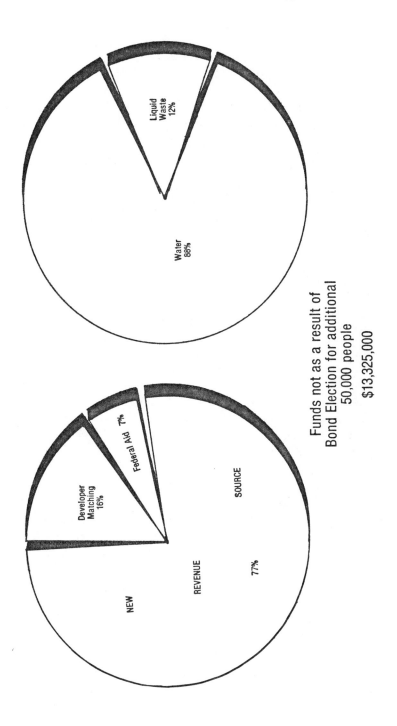

Liquid
Waste
12%

Water
88%

NEW
REVENUE
SOURCE
77%

Developer
Matching
16%

Federal Aid 7%

Funds not as a result of
Bond Election for additional
50,000 people
$13,325,000

CAPTAL IMPROVEMENTS PROGRAM
USES OF GENERAL OBLIGATION BONDS

$20,729,383

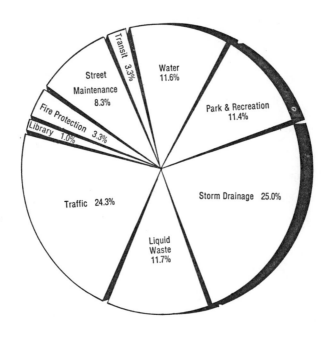

Transit 3.3%

Water
11.6%

Street
Maintenance
8.3%

Fire Protection 3.3%

Library 1.0%

Park & Recreation
11.4%

Traffic 24.3%

Storm Drainage 25.0%

Liquid
Waste
11.7%

CAPITAL IMPROVEMENTS PROGRAM

SOURCES AND USES OF FUNDS**

1974 ELECTION

DEPARTMENT	G. O. BONDS	REVENUE BONDS	FEDERAL AID	STATE AID	SPECIAL ASSESSMENTS	CURRENT & MISC. REVENUE	TOTAL
Environmental Health	$25,000 100.0% .1%						$25,000 100.0% .0%
Fire	$686,983 100.0% 3.3%						$686,983 100.0% 1.1%
Library	$200,000 100.0% 1.0%						$200,000 100.0% .3%
Parks	$2,357,000 46.8% 11.4%		$2,024,500 40.2% 11.1%			$657,500 13.0% 10.2%	$5,039,000 100.0% 7.8%
Public Buildings		$6,300,000 66.3% 77.4%				$3,200,000 33.7% 49.9%	$9,500,000 100.0% 14.8%
Public Works	($16,767,400)* (46.0%) (80.9%)		($10,160,000) (27.9%) (55.5%)	($2,196,200) (6.0%) (100.0%)	($6,356,500) (17.5%) (74.3%)	($951,000) (2.6%) (14.8%)	($36,431,000) (100.0%) (56.6%)
Liquid Waste	$2,425,000 23.3% 11.7%		$5,750,000 55.2% 31.4%	$625,000 6.0% 28.5%	$1,625,000 15.6% 19.0%		$10,425,000 100.0% 16.2%
Storm Drainage	$5,180,000 100.0% 25.0%						$5,180,000 100.0% 8.1%
Street Maintenance	$1,730,500 91.7% 8.3%					$157,000 8.3% 2.4%	$1,887,500 100.0% 2.9%
Traffic	$5,036,900 33.3% 24.3%		$4,410,000 29.1% 24.1%	$1,571,200 10.4% 71.5%	$3,331,500 22.0% 38.9%	$794,000 5.2% 12.4%	$15,143,600 100.0% 23.5%
Water	$2,395,000 63.1% 11.6%				$1,400,000 36.9% 16.4%		$3,795,000 100.0% 5.9%
Services		$75,000 6.3% .9%				$1,120,000 93.7% 17.5%	$1,195,000 100.0% 1.9%
Transportation Aviation			$2,211,665 39.5% 25.8%	$3,341,885 59.7% 18.3%		$45,350 .8% .8%	$5,598,900 100.0% 8.7%
Parking					$2,200,000 100.0% 25.7%		$2,200,000 100.0% 3.4%
Transit	$693,000 20.0% 3.3%		$2,772,000 80.0% 15.1%				$3,465,000 100.0% 5.4%
TOTAL	$20,729,383 32.2% 100.0%	$8,586,665 13.3% 100.0%	$18,298,385 28.4% 100.0%	$2,196,200 3.4% 100.0%	$8,556,500 13.3% 100.0%	$5,973,850 9.3% 100.0%	$64,340,983 100.0% 100.0%

* Parentheses indicates a subtotal of Public Works Divisions
** The first percentage under the dollar amount indicates the distribution of a department's sources of revenue
The second percentage under each dollar amount indicates the distribution of usage by department of each revenue source.

Bibliography

Albuquerque, *Capital Improvements Program* (Albuquerque/Bernalillo County Planning Department, 1974).

————, *Policies Plan* (Albuquerque/Bernalillo County Planning Department, 1974).

American Institute of Planners, *The Law of Planning and Land Use: Regulation in Colorado* (Denver: Colorado Chapter of AIP, 1975)

Aronson, J. Richard, and Schwartz, Eli (eds.), *Management Policies in Local Government Finance* (Washington, D.C.: International City Management Association, 1975).

Altshuler, Alan A., *The City Planning Process* (Ithaca, New York: Cornell University Press, 1965).

Bair, Fred H., Jr., *Planning Cities* (Chicago: American Society of Planning Officials, 1970).

Bucks County, Pennsylvania, *Performance Zoning* (Doylestown: Bucks County Planning Commission, 1973).

Catanese, Anthony James, *Planners and Local Politics: Impossible Dreams* (Beverly Hills, California: Sage Publications, 1974).

Denver, *Capital Improvements Financing, 1976-1990* (Department of Planning, City and County of Denver, 1976).

————, *Planning Toward the Future: A Comprehensive Plan for Denver* (Department of Planning, City and County of Denver, 1978).

Downes, Bryan T., *Politics, Change, and the Urban Crisis* (North Scituate, Massachusetts: Duxbury Press, 1976).

Friedmann, John Rembert Peter, *Retracking America: A Theory of Transactive Planning* (Garden City, New York: Anchor Press, 1973).

Gallion, Arthur B., and Eisner, Simon, *The Urban Pattern* (New York City: The D. Van Nostrand Co., 3rd ed. 1975).

Gans, Herbert J., *The Levittowners: Ways of Life and Politics in a New Suburban Community* (New York City: Vintage Books, 1967).

Goodman, Robert, *After the Planners* (New York City: Simon and Schuster, 1971).

Goodman, William I., and Freund, Eric C. (eds.), *Principles and Practice of Urban Planning* (Washington, D.C.: International City Management Association, 4th ed. 1968).

Havlick, Spenser W., *The Urban Organism: The City's Natural Resources from an Environmental Perspective* (New York City: Macmillan Publishing Co., 1974).

Harman, Douglas, *On the Joys of Being Manager* (Washington, D.C.: International City Management Association, 1973).

Healy, Robert G., *Land Use and the States* (Washington, D.C.: Resources for the Future, Inc., 1976).

Hester, Herschel G., III, *Planning and Zoning Administration in Utah* (Salt Lake City: Utah League of Cities and Towns, 1977).

Higbee, Edward, *The Squeeze: Cities Without Space* (New York City: William Morrow & Co., 1960).

Jacobs, Jane, *The Death and Life of Great American Cities* (New York City: Random House, 1961).

Kahn, Si, *How People Get Power: Organizing Oppressed Communities for Action* (New York City: McGraw-Hill Book Co., 1970).

McLean, Mary (ed.), *Local Planning Administration* (Chicago: International City Management Association, 3rd ed. 1959).

Maxwell, James A., and Aronson, J. Richard., *Financing State and Local Governments* (Washington, D.C.: The Brookings Institution, 1977).

Saarinen, Thomas F., *Environmental Planning: Perception and Behavior* (Boston: Houghton Mifflin Co., 1976).

Scott, Mel, *American City Planning* (Berkeley: University of California Press, 1969).

Smith, Herbert H., *The Citizen's Guide to Zoning* (West Trenton, New Jersey: Chandler-Davis Publishing Co., 1965).

Stedman, Murray S., Jr., *Urban Politics* (Cambridge, Massachusetts: Winthrop Publishers, 2nd ed. 1975).

Walker, Robert A., *The Planning Function in Urban Government* (Chicago: The University of Chicago Press, 1941).

U.S. Department of Commerce, *A Standard State Planning Enabling Act* (Washington, D.C.: U.S. Government Printing Office, 1928).

U.S. Department of Commerce, *A Standard State Zoning Enabling Act* (Washington, D.C.: U.S. Government Printing Office, 1926).

Index

References in this index will lead the reader to pages where either the topic is mentioned briefly or substantial treatment of the subject begins. The reader is advised to examine portions of the text preceding and following these reference points and to consult the "Table of Contents" generally.

in preparation of 62, form and format 63, and subdivision control 86

McFall, Trudy, 157

metropolitan areas, 147, *see also* community development; urban design; urban renewal

Milwaukee (Wisconsin), 15

Minneapolis (Minnesota), 150, 157

"Model Cities" program, 21, 43, 116, 165

models, 16, 39, planning commission by-laws 48, state enabling legislation, 56, 66

"muckrakers," 14

National Conference on City Planning, First, 15

National Institute of Municipal Attorneys, 87

National Resources Planning Board (NRPB), 17

neighborhoods, role in planning ix, 29, 30, 63

New Communities Act of 1968, 21, 116

New Jersey, 1953 planning enabling act quoted 56

New York City, 150, Commission Plan of 1811 13, 1916 zoning ordinance 16, 72

Office of Management and Budget, Federal (OMB), A-95 review process 62, 157, 163

O'Harrow, Dennis, quoted 117

"Operation Breakthrough," 21, 116

Patterson (New Jersey), 98

Philadelphia (Pennsylvania), 13, 94, 150

Phoenix (Arizona), 94

planned unit development (PUD), 89, 122, 167, and growth management 151

planners, professional, Chapter 9 (including questions of "professionalism," neighborhood and advocacy planning, use of staff versus consultants), and the planning commission 100, citizen questions concerning 104

planning, need for vii, 4, and democracy x, 22, reasons for 1, unconcern for 7, lack of understanding of 7, citizen involvement in 11, 34, historical development of 12, shortcomings of as a profession 25, definitions of 27, tools of 31, and politics 39, allocating the functions and responsibilities of 44, development of as a profession 98

planning, programming, budgeting system (PPBS), 45, 166

planning commission, planning board, Chapter 4 (including general organization theory, structure, functions, questions of advisory versus management role), vii, establishment of 29, and elected bodies 38, and the master plan and subdivision controls 46, relationship to governing body 49, member characteristics 51, and zoning 76, and planning professionals 100,

/307.765649(1979>(1/

MAR 27 1995

MAY 10 1995

DATE DUE